PETS ARE FAMILY

It's as simple as that.

ERIKA SINNER

To

My husband Chris and my kids Kingston, Mishka, Edmond, and Theodore who have shown me the profound depths of love.

And to Mallory Cash who has consistently held space for my heart, offering unwavering support and understanding.

And to my family, friends, and extraordinary community on social media whose boundless strength has guided us through the challenges we've faced.

And to Nora Flansburg, Thomas McGuire, Ryan Rausch, Anne Marie White, and my dedicated team for their support, enabling me to embark on a healing path, prioritize Edmond's cancer treatment, and fulfill my purpose in writing this book.

And to Audrey Wu, a steadfast and devoted friend who has stood by my side through thick and thin. She has been there for me in countless ways that words fail to capture adequately.

To the University of Illinois, Creve Coeur Animal Hospital, and their entire teams for their urgency, love, care and support. They are treasures beyond measure, and I will forever cherish them.

And to you, the reader –

Regardless of why you are here, whether to find some comfort in your own grief, to support someone dear to you, or to simply immerse yourself in a story of love …to you, I say, I have thought about you at every step of writing this book.

Pets are Family
It's as simple as that.

print ISBN: 979-8-35094-540-9
ebook ISBN: 979-8-35093-635-3

"Erika displays courageous vulnerability in this book and exemplifies how necessary it is in our grief journey. This is a passionate guide through pet loss that takes time to address both the emotional as well as the practical aspects of the subject matter, some of which have yet to be addressed in current literature."

- Christiana Saia, GC-C, Certified Pet Loss Coach, Lap of Love Veterinary Hospice

"In 'Pets are Family,' Erika beautifully captures the profound impact of pets who have a permanent residence in our hearts. This exploration of grief, resilience, unconditional love and companionship reminds us that we are not alone in experiencing the loss of a beloved pet. As I personally embark on the final chapter in the life of our own furry family member, Erika reminds us that the bond we share never goes away and will always be cherished in their everlasting memories."

– Greg Divis, Chief Executive Officer

"The conversation regarding the composition of our "family" often neglects, including those that many of us can't fathom life without – our pets. We fully share the most intimate aspects of ourselves and our lives with our pets that are otherwise reserved for few, if any, human beings. Through their unconditional love, our pets fill the cracks within us and enrich our souls, while creating an indelible mark on our hearts. Due to this extraordinary bond, the final stages of our physical time together can be filled with turmoil, intense grief and even despair. Through her own experiences, Erika helps us better understand this journey and ignites a powerful conversation of how we are failing to properly recognize that pets are just as critical to a family unit as human beings, while offering advice and resources regarding how we can do better."

- CG Hintmann, Esq, General Counsel and Chief Compliance Officer

"In my lifetime, I have lost many pets due to critical illnesses and have suffered a great deal of grief from losing what I consider to be family members. Our animals do not have the same life span as humans so to endure these losses can take a toll on the entire family. Yet, humans continue to adopt new animals into their lives because pets provide unconditional love and much joy to us. Erika has also suffered a great loss for her beloved Kingston and discusses her grief and the impact it has had not only at home, but also in the workplace. With this grief, Erika was inspired to write this amazing book which sparks the conversation on how we as humans can deal with these losses, but also what we can do differently in society to support this grief that is sometimes disregarded."

- *Melissa Hughes, Chief Operating Officer and former Director,*
Human Resources St. Louis Cardinals

Contents

CONTENT WARNING

The contents of this book are emotionally and intellectually challenging to engage with. The author's intent is to create a space where we can engage bravely, empathetically, and thoughtfully with difficult content. However, references to mental health and sexual abuse in Part 1 and mention of death/illness of pets throughout may not be suitable for some readers.

If you or someone you know is struggling with mental health or suicidal thoughts, please seek help.

Call 1-800-273-TALK (8255) and you'll be directed to a trained counselor at a crisis center near you, 24/7.

FORWARD

Pets are family.

You're probably nodding along. It's the kind of statement that is short, sweet, and built for connecting with others. Almost 70% of U.S. households include a pet[1]. Whether you care for a pet directly, on a day-to-day basis – or you've seen the mutual devotion between a loved one and their pet – a pet is likely part of your life.

You may also have experienced and witnessed the pain when the time has come to say goodbye to pets. Whether that time can be planned for or comes unexpectedly, it is stunning in its cruelty and a poignant reminder of the loss that is inherently part of loving another soul.

Pets are family. It's as simple as that.

Or is it?

The author of this book, Erika Sinner, came to a realization that is profound in its truth:

If pets are family …

… then when the time comes to mourn their passing …

… why are the resources and structures to support families in that loss so inadequate?

My first experience with pet loss was a textbook case of how NOT to properly process grief. While my heart hurt, and I couldn't stop thinking about her final hours, I put on a brave face, showed up to work, and acted as if her passing was a minor blip.

---

1 *https://www.forbes.com/advisor/pet-insurance/pet-ownership-statistics/#:~:-text=at%20a%20Glance-,66%25%20of%20U.S.%20households%20(86.9%20million%20homes)%20own%20a,fish%20(11.1%20million%20households

I mentioned it to a few colleagues and brushed off their attempts to provide sympathy or condolence. But when I was alone, I would wonder where her soul was and if she was okay.

Eventually, I buried the pain right alongside other painful episodes in my life, covering all of it up with a sunny attitude and lots of achievements. It was such a hard experience that it gave me pause when my family considered opening our hearts to a new pup (who is now a treasured member of our family).

We could have quite a chat about what it took to properly heal all that pain. In fact, you're about to experience that kind of chat.

Fifteen years ago, I met Erika on my first day in a new job. Erika and I became friends right away. It didn't take me long to see that the things that were immediately apparent – her friendly demeanor, her candor, and her interest in helping me to succeed – were the outward manifestation of a person whose character and values resonated deeply with me.

Erika is a person you want to have in your corner: both when the shit hits the fan, AND when you are the shit. While the circumstances that brought this book to you may be painful, I am heartened that you are about to get to know a very special person. Erika has shown great bravery and vulnerability in sharing about the numerous losses that she experienced in her life – any one of which would have been incredibly challenging to overcome – before the loss that inspired her to write this book. As with any loss, the wound associated with losing a pet needs to heal properly. Recognizing the wound is the first step.

When Erika and her husband, Chris, lost Kingston, it was very painful for me to witness the blow-by-blow as documented in their social media posts. While Erika and I have supported each other through some of the most challenging situations that life can deliver, I didn't know what to do to alleviate her pain. One thing Erika and I both value is showing up – being there for each other in person. We catch planes the same way we catch Ubers and Lyfts, so the 2,000-mile distance between us is not a barrier. But I sensed, in this case, that showing up in person was the last thing she and Chris needed or wanted from me.

As the days and weeks passed, though, a few things came forward to me that I was moved to share with Erika. My hand would start placing the order or sending a text even while my mind was saying, *"She has 40,000 followers on social media. Someone has probably already sent her that ..."*

There were other times when my mind would say, *"You should send her that,"* and my hand would stop me.

Reading about these instances in the context of Erika's narrative has been, to say the least, remarkable. I now see that my nephew Kingston is teaching me how to show up for Erika in a different way. I am deeply humbled that he recognizes the strength of my bond with Erika and has continued to make his quiet, regal presence known to me.

I, too, suffered a loss when Kingston passed. It is quite a jolt to realize just how inadequate our structures are for something so many of us will experience.

Erika is a person who will empathize with your pain while helping you to figure out the action that is your right next step. This book is vintage Erika: you will connect with her, and then you'll know what action to take when you are faced with similar circumstances. You may not know what to do or what to say, so Erika has even provided examples of text messages and scripts so you don't have to start from scratch. That's Erika.

Given that so many of us will go through this experience, I believe this book will inspire action for long overdue changes that recognize and affirm the role that pets play in our lives.

Because pets are family.

It's as simple as that.

Audrey Wu (Pictured with Autumn)
August 2023

INTRODUCTION

In the darkness of my mind, as I lay down to sleep on the night of June 4, 2023, a haunting thought crossed my mind: Maybe I just won't wake up tomorrow. The idea of slipping away peacefully in my sleep felt like a gift, a release from the overwhelming weight of my emotions. The thought of never opening my eyes again, seemed like a merciful escape. I mustered the courage to schedule an appointment with my doctor the very next day. There was a single opening available at 2pm, and I took it. The day I sat in that exam room, a mixture of grief and shame was coursing through my veins, as I prepared to reveal the extent of my struggle, and how deeply impacted I was by the loss of my beloved dog, Kingston. The internet Google gods were not there for me. The advice to work out, try to sleep, listen to music, stay in a routine… none of it was helping.

Before I continue, I want to acknowledge the extreme privilege from which I write. Many of you reading this have endured far greater hardships, struggles, experiences, and traumas than I have. This is my story, and I hope that by sharing it, I can help others feel seen, loved, and understood. So, here we go.

I am a CEO and the proud founder of a thriving company; I'm in a deeply committed loving relationship; and I have ambitious dreams still to be realized. But how did I get here? Before delving into the most challenging ordeal of my life, it is important to provide context for who I am and the life I have led. I hope by understanding my journey it will shed light on why I am so passionate about validating the traumatic experience of losing a pet. For those who have never experienced this type of loss, it is critical to comprehend that the pain runs deep. While I may not have endured all the evils of the world, I have faced my fair share of hardships. By being vulnerable and sharing those experiences with you, I hope to convey the gravity of the grief that consumed me and affirm that losing a pet is a profoundly agonizing experience, just as it can be to lose a human loved one. My purpose in sharing my story is to help those who are suffering from pet loss and those who wish to support someone on this journey to understand the genuine impact of losing a pet.

I do not think of myself as an author, but I have chosen to write this book. My life alone may not be interesting enough to share with the world, but I believe what Kingston has taught me is. To adequately convey those lessons, I knew I needed to let you into my life. I have considered the vulnerability of putting myself out there in this way. Will I be able to handle the inherent feedback that comes this type of openness? Yet, what I truly believe is we cannot "normalize" something if we don't talk about it.

Throughout my life, I have been learning how to find importance in the world. To truly believe in my own self-worth without the constant need for validation. To feel that I belong here simply because I am me, and to understand that I matter without any expectations or conditions. Maybe for me, it was my dad choosing the "other woman" and the life he was living in parallel to ours when I was seven, or my mom's decision to uproot us from Texas to a small Midwestern Missouri town, with little knowledge of the place and struggling to learn English. It could be the trauma of surviving sexual abuse and having a family that chose forgiveness over advocacy. Perhaps it was the failure of my marriage to my high school sweetheart or the brief second marriage that led to a cross-country move and a return to Missouri. These experiences made me realize that this is MY life, and every decision I make is shaped by my own unique circumstances and thoughts on how to navigate. We all do our best with the information available to us at any given time and follow our instincts. In light of this, I've learned the importance of taking ownership of my feelings and actions, embracing them as part of my journey, and continuing to move forward.

Most could label my life a success: I'm a Mexican-American woman who founded and runs a multimillion-dollar company, lives in a million-dollar home, married her best friend and decided kids were not for her...instead, has four Shar Pei; now three. Yet, it has taken until the age of 38 for me to begin filling the void inside myself, to accept that I matter just as I am. That means, I'm important enough to **honor** my feelings. My first thought is how could it have taken this long? My second was, it can't just be me who feels this way.

I am only now just beginning to grasp the importance of respecting and cherishing the privilege of living this life. No one can live it for you, and no one can feel for you, and nothing can numb pain. So, here I am, ready to embark on this journey of sharing my story, my experiences, and the profound impact that losing my dog Kingston has had on my life. May my vulnerability, honesty, and empathy for others illuminate a path of understanding and healing. Together, let us explore the depths of grief and find comfort in the power of love and compassion.

A wise friend, Thomas, gave me sage advice when I was confined to my bed recovering from an ankle break. He said, "There is no going around it, the pain. You must go through it." I feel I've been "going through it" my whole life. I had made it through so much, that I believed I could handle, well, anything. Yet, here in the depths of despair, I found myself questioning the value of waking up to another day.

As a CEO leading a flourishing company, I had navigated life's challenges with a sense of confidence, believing I could handle anything that came my way. However, the passing of Kingston shattered that illusion. I found myself plunged into a realm of profound grief; unlike anything I had experienced before. It wasn't just an ache in my heart; it was a pain that engulfed every fiber of my being. The weight of this grief brought me to my knees, and I found myself screaming into pillows, desperate to muffle the raw and animalistic sounds escaping from within me. The intensity of the emotions I felt was overwhelming.

It was a grief that brought forth uncontrollable sobs, leaving me breathless and on the verge of hyperventilation. A grief that engulfed me, so unrelenting and unforgiving. Eventually overwhelming my body's nervous system, resulting in a projectile vomit during a hot yoga session. My body seemed to rebel against my attempts to suppress the pain, demanding that I acknowledge and honor my grief. It was as if my own body screamed at me, commanding me to retreat to my bed and surrender to the depths of my sorrow.

Yet, I resisted, attempting to carry on with life as if nothing had changed. Yes, I shed tears in those vulnerable moments on the floor when it all bubbled out, but I also threw myself into intense workouts, delved into research on the cancer that took Kingston from me, blamed myself for not detecting it earlier, and buried myself in work…for a good seventeen days…that is all it took for my body to say no more.

That morning coming home from yoga having vomited, sobbing and trembling the whole way home, I still was thinking about how I could delay a meeting that morning and work the rest of the day. I was fighting my body's need to grieve, but as I crawled into bed and clutched a heating pad to soothe my aching stomach, the weight of shame settled upon me. Shame that it hurt this much. Shame that my team would not think I was strong. People lose loved ones every single day. How could I be this immobile and unfunctional? I knew I felt all of it inside, but now it was showing externally. It became clear there was no other option than to cancel that Friday's meetings and take the day off. I couldn't even bring myself to text my leadership team; it was my husband who had to deliver the message. This was the second time I would be asking my team to rearrange my day and reschedule meetings in the last two weeks.

It had been seventeen days since the nightmare began. The six days of trying to save Kingston and then eleven days since he passed.

That Friday June 2nd projectile vomit combined with the thoughts I started having that weekend led to Monday, June 5th, going to my doctor's appointment to talk about my mental health. I was told that "yes, this is hard, but let's see how we can manage." Some of the questions I received felt off. I wanted to say, "If I had just lost a human son would you be asking the same thing?" I felt my doctor was trying to navigate what seemed like uncharted waters, but also, was taken aback by how unstable I seemed. I've been going to this practice for fifteen years and had always presented stable and in control. My doctor and I made a short-term plan that included prescriptions and a follow up action of my making a therapist appointment.

I felt heard in the acknowledgment my body was clearly going through severe stress. I started to feel proud that I honored my feelings and sought help. I called to make a therapy appointment, but before even meeting with a therapist, I knew I needed to get these new feelings out. That is when I started writing. These words just poured out of me. This level of pain and grief…how could it be more than anything else I had felt in my life? Even as the CEO of my own company, I found myself grappling with shame over how profoundly pet loss was affecting me and the need to take time off to grieve. It made me realize that if I, in my position, could feel this way, then others must undoubtedly experience similar emotions, perhaps with even more weight, especially when they don't have the flexibility to take time off, and policies may not explicitly address pet loss in the same way they do for human loss.

For our family, our story only got worse. The day after my doctor's appointment Edmond, our blue Shar Pei, was scheduled to go in for X-rays on his back legs for suspected arthritis and a possible need for surgery. I was nervous about anesthesia, but knew it had to be done. They were going to go ahead and clean his teeth while they had him under. I was working that day. Day 21 since this nightmare began and I received the call that they had found a dime size tumor on his tongue and had to remove it. It felt as though the air was sucked out of my body, leaving me breathless. My husband and I went to pick up Edmond, only to be informed that the tumor had to be sent to a lab to confirm if it was benign or cancer. Six days of torment lay ahead, as we simultaneously processed Kingston's passing. That was the day my team proactively cleared my calendar for the rest of the week. They weren't even aware of my doctor's visit the day before. They knew before I did that my entire focus needed to be on my family.

June 12th finally arrived, and the call came. Cancer. Aggressive cancer. My heart was still struggling to reconcile the fact that I would never hold Kingston again, and now we were thrust into a battle to save Edmond. Twenty-seven days at this point, of intense stress and pain, and this news shut me down. I completely melted down in my living room after receiving the call, back to the same level of pain I had felt the day I lost Kingston. The familiar sound of muffled screaming only to realize it was me and that I was on the floor, again. After collapsing in my living room, my tears flowing uncontrollably, my body heaving with pain, I experienced a surge of rage. The tears seemed to have an off switch, and my mind directed all energy towards standing up, propelled by sheer determination. I thought clearly in a tunnel vision sort of way. For the first time, I made a firm decision not to feel shame or judgment about prioritizing my well-being and focusing on my family's needs. With a trembling hand, I picked up my phone and texted my team, expressing my uncertainty about the future and when I would be able to return to work that week. All I knew was that I had to find an oncologist. By the time you read these words, that part of our journey will have unfolded, and I pray from the depths of my being that it all went well. I envision a future where I am smiling and cuddling all my kids.

This brings me back to the purpose of writing this book. In today's society, we're not entirely comfortable with grief or sharing our emotions. There's an unspoken pressure to move past sorrow, aiming for a quick return to normalcy. When a human family member passes, we do have some established rituals to honor their memory. Obituaries, ceremonies, funerals, sending flowers, and donating to charities are all recognized ways to pay tribute to a person's life. However, when it comes to our beloved pets, the landscape is different. There's an even greater lack of established rituals or societal norms to guide us through the grieving process. We often struggle to find the right words or actions to express our condolences or commemorate the life of a cherished loved one. The absence of established norms can leave families that include pets feeling isolated in their grief, unsure of how to express their feelings or commemorate their furry family member's life in a meaningful way.

Even within my own company, where I have always had a focus not only on pets, but also prioritizing human beings first; knowing we are all so much more than our job titles and what we do for a living. Yet, there were still misunderstandings on how to support me and my emotions upon my return. I learned quickly after speaking with some of my team that no one really knows what to do when someone loses a pet. They don't know if they should send flowers, or if they should reach out, or give you space. I think this can be true in all grief, but even more gray for pets.

This realization prompted me to ask: How can this be? Our pets are woven into the fabric of our everyday lives. There are routines, memories made, some pets even sleep in their "parents" bed (like ours). How do you get any more connected than that? When a pet passes, you are left feeling a void so big. The silence in your house is deafening. Your own home feels like a death trap because at any moment one of the hundreds of memories can gut punch you and bring you to your knees. Pets are sources of unconditional love, companionship, and cherished memories.

We need to validate the grief of losing a pet, to acknowledge that it's okay to need time off work, to cancel plans, and that grief knows no timeline. It's okay to take the time we need, even if it means letting others down. We can honor and validate our feelings for our beloved pets, just as we would for any other family member.

It's having the realization and understanding that pets are family. It is as simple as that. Once we accept this truth, the grief, the pain, and the need for time off work all make sense. If others could acknowledge this truth, then our societal norms surrounding loss would apply. I knew I had to write, to raise awareness, to provide resources, and to share what guides us through grief of this magnitude: love, kindness, and community.

And so now, as a non-author, writer, any of those labels, I'm not concerned about how my writing comes off, if there are run on sentences, if you are or are not supposed to include photos weaved in and out of stories, if books are supposed to be structured in a certain way....none of it. What matters is that I authentically share my experiences, emotions, and journey, in the hope of connecting with you, the reader. I knew that you might be going through this painful experience right now, and my words would let you know that you are not alone. If you are reading this to learn how to support someone who is grieving the loss of a pet, I hope to offer you a glimpse into the magnitude of their pain.

This book is not meant to be read from start to finish, although I hope you do. I've poured my heart and soul into these pages. This book is meant to help you in whatever way you need right now. Being a person of action, I knew this book could not just be me sharing my story. It needed to include actionable things you could use as a person experiencing grief or as the person trying to love and support someone going through it. That is why I have also created resources found in Part 5.

I believe there is more we can do beyond validating feelings, offering ways to support family and friends suffering loss, but also the surround. First to extend support to the veterinary community and their offices, who already carry immense responsibility. Second, the area I am most passionate about, is providing space to breathe. By this I mean the inclusion of pets as part of an organization's bereavement policy. As an employer myself, from the day I founded my company, we've had pet bereavement incorporated. This has always been commented on as something special and "different". Pet bereavement leave is often overlooked or absent from organizational policies. Yet, after having my own experience and trying to return to work, I realized this must become the standard. I believe by raising awareness and providing resources to help support those conversations, we can make a difference. Additionally, we need to support employers in welcoming their employees back after experiencing this type of grief, whether it's through easing them back into work or providing resources to managers and teammates on how to offer support.

Losing Kingston illuminated for me my responsibility in this mission. You'll discover if you read Part 2, I have been given clues along the way, but his passing propelled me to act. A calling on my heart was placed that I've tried to ignore, but the call became louder. Pets *are* **family**.

Every day following the loss of Kingston, you, dear reader, have taken over my thoughts. I knew you were out there, either experiencing the same emotions I was, or loving someone who has lost a pet, yet unsure of how to provide comfort. This book is for you. I am not an experienced author, an influencer, or a qualified psychologist offering advice on grief. I am simply a person who has walked this path, sharing my own experiences and emotions in the hopes it would help someone else. I am taking a leap of faith, casting aside fear and embracing vulnerability to start an important conversation. My goal is for us to get more comfortable honoring our feelings and leaning on each other as we move forward.

Here is a map for how to think about this book.

Part 1 is getting to know me and my story. It sheds light on how we judge ourselves and others when only the person who knows the depth of pain is the person experiencing the pain.

Part 2 is falling in love with our family and fur kids (and hopefully by the end of reading this section you'll accept the term kids without the prerequisite of "fur").

Part 3 delves into the experience of being told that you are losing your furry loved one and the journey that unfolds when faced with the "gift" of euthanasia. If you are supporting someone going through this but find it difficult to comprehend the intensity of their pain or the trauma they endure, this section will offer insight.

For you, dear reader, currently having to make the extraordinarily difficult decision to end your pet's suffering, this will hurt. It will hurt a lot, but I hope through reading about our experience, you will be better equipped to navigate this challenging path.

If you've already gone through this experience, I hope this validates every single feeling you have on how horrible it was and that yes, it was and is trauma.

Part 4 explores why this conversation matters and highlights the significance of the resources I created to support you and others.

Part 5 is the action. None of these are meant to be a playbook for how to best handle pain or as a magical solution to make it all disappear. Instead, these tools are meant to inspire thinking, considerations, and encourage you to lean in with love for your friends and family going through this, or if you are going through a hard time; how to ask for help and lean on them.

Together, let us honor our pets as family and the love they bring into our lives. Let us create a world that acknowledges the profound impact of pet loss and supports one another with empathy and understanding.

PART 1:

SELF-DISCOVERY

1

The Unseen Hurt: Experiencing Beyond Assumptions

In August 2018, after an incredible Peloton ride, I came flying down the stairs high on endorphins, energy, and eager to start on a new project I just landed. I was being hired on as a consultant a month after being fired or given the "opportunity" to resign from my current role where I had poured my heart and soul into building an organization, creating a market, and successfully launching a pharmaceutical medication. I was determined to prove that I was back on my feet; until I wasn't.

I was flat on my ass at the bottom of the stairs looking up at the ceiling with my pups surrounding me. They formed a perfect 4-point perimeter blockade around me knowing I was hurt. I was grateful that somehow, in the midst of the fall, my phone had landed on my chest, allowing me to call my husband for help. I hesitated to dial 911; how would they get in? Break down my door? My Shar Pei would go insane. In hindsight, I probably should have. They give you pain meds on the way to the ER, but the ER, FYI, does not until they confirm, by X-ray, and prove the ankle is broken. This is due to a national opioid crisis, which I'm proud to say in my line of work, I'm directly working on addressing.

Every part of this experience exceeded my expectations in the worst way possible. Instead of a simple cast and discharge, I found myself referred to an orthopedic surgeon. I expected the surgeon to say that I would need minor surgery or maybe just to "set it". Instead,

I was confronted with the reality of major surgery. The procedure involved an open reduction and internal fixation (ORIF), requiring 2 screws and a plate. However, during the surgery it became evident that I needed six screws, a larger plate and to open the right side of the ankle to reattach a ligament I snapped. (Yes, still talking about the result of just coming down the stairs.) I would also need a second surgery to remove the stabilizing syndesmotic hardware 12 weeks later, and the rest of the hardware would stay in the rest of my life.

What the actual hell? Not only did I find myself unemployed, but now I couldn't even walk. It seemed like a cruel joke. For six weeks, I was not allowed to put any weight on my injured ankle, followed by eight weeks of physical therapy. During those initial six weeks, I had to rely on others for basic tasks like getting to the bathroom, fetching water, and waiting for food. The nerve pain was excruciating, and I was confined to my bedroom. My husband promised to assist me with showering every day, despite the challenges. I had read on a blog that when you break your ankle, certain things like skipping showers become inevitable and you may smell. But I passionately rejected that notion.

Sitting on the cold shower floor, feeling the water cleanse me, brought a profound sense of relief. Tears streamed down my face. I tried not to cry out while my husband helped me back in bed. I was proud the shower was happening. I felt fresh, but still not okay emotionally. I was frustrated. I just had to BE WITH MYSELF and *feel* it all. I couldn't out work or outsmart the pain to regain control, I couldn't distract myself because I was physically stuck in place.

This is where love poured in. My friend, Stephanie, a fellow Shar Pei mom whom we met on Instagram, came up from Austin, TX and stayed a week. Others dropped off food or fun care packages. Flowers were arriving daily. My bedroom could have been a pop-up flower shop on a New York City corner.

I pushed through the physical and emotional pain, finding a renewed sense of focus. I knew that others had experienced far worse situations than losing a job and suffering a single ankle break. It was time to end the pity party. I began inviting friends over. I also asked my husband to help me bring my computer to bed instead of relying solely on my phone. I had used technology as an escape and a means to numb myself with social media and the internet. But now, I shifted my focus to my present reality. What did I love to do? How did I want to move forward professionally? What had I dreamed of? My ankle break occurred on August 11th, 2018. Just four months later, my company was launched with three clients on board. By January, I had hired my first employee, followed by two more in February.

Instead of working as a lone marketer contracted to help a single organization bring a vital medication to market, I realized that I could teach others to do what I had done and scale our impact. This approach would enable us to assist numerous organizations. The healthcare space is filled with innovation from incredibly talented scientists and doctors. However, the experience of commercializing these advancements doesn't always align. As small to midsize companies secure funding, they often face limitations. Investors approve only a limited number of full-time employees to execute operations, leaving little room for dedicated sales and marketing budgets. Therefore, companies struggle to access top talent. Some of the medicines we work on are lifesaving. By launching this new model, I believed we could make a difference. If it were your daughter, friend, parent, or yourself needing a certain medication, you would hope someone is fighting for them.

It is not easy starting a company. I don't mean to oversimplify. Lots of lessons learned, support from friends, hard work, and the sage advice, "always have to push through" – no short cuts.

Despite multiple surgeries and extensive physical therapy, my ankle never felt quite right. Each plane trip, even with compression socks, would cause swelling and pain to flare up. I pushed through, wearing flats instead of heels and questioning how I had ever managed airports, conventions, sales meetings, and client visits while enduring the discomfort. I kept my head held high and determined.

My life picked up again and my calendar overflowed with meetings, weekly trips, and 70-hour work weeks. If my sense of self-worth and fulfillment were derived from my professional achievements, then it was brimming to the brim.

Then, on February 19, 2020, after a grueling four-hour flight to San Diego, my ankle ignited with pain. I made it to my hotel room and noticed a substantial lump on the left side where the hardware remained. The following day, I pushed through a 12-hour client day and made it to my return flight home on Friday. I emailed my orthopedic surgeon to schedule a follow-up on that flight.

If the universe had been attempting to send me a message about slowing down, with the ankle break causing me to miss out on my first consulting job and jump back into a full workload that would have demanded 80-hour weeks, it was now delivering a resounding verdict. Did I really intend to maintain 70-hour work weeks and travel incessantly for 22 weeks straight? The surgeon confirmed that the hardware in my ankle had loosened, resulting in the development of a cyst and the nerve pain I was experiencing. Surgery was necessary to remove all the hardware and repair the damaged nerve. I couldn't believe it. I had finally settled into a routine, incorporating consistent workouts, and even had moments where I forgot I had broken my ankle in the first place. And now, I was facing another surgery.

The procedure was scheduled, only to be cancelled a day before due to the pandemic that swept the world—COVID-19. All surgeries nationally were cancelled, unless an emergency in other words, "only if a bone is coming out." The world entered the fight with a pandemic. It wasn't until a month later, when hospitals implemented safety protocols, that I finally had the hardware removed.

The waiting was tough. The days when the nerve would be caught on hardware were debilitating. Planning time off for surgery around a client launch was hard, and planning for the healing process was frustrating. Yet I knew; I had seen this movie before. Time to put my head down and push through. There was no escaping it.

The day of the surgery was tough, with COVID protocols in place, temperature checks, and being escorted to the back alone. I entered the same cold bathroom as before, undressed, and donned the blue gown. Placing my clothes and shoes into a plastic bag that eerily resembled the belongings bag on crime shows in the morgue, I couldn't help but feel uneasy about the impending surgery and general anesthesia. "I can't believe I'm here again," I thought as I put on the gown, booties, and hairnet, and climbed onto the assigned bed. I waited, watching the seconds tick away on the black and white clock, reminiscent of the clocks I used to stare at in high school. Despite my right leg shaking uncontrollably under the white blanket, in the sterile holding room, I tried to maintain calmness. I wore a white N95 mask, mailed to me by a friend, that was a requirement until entering the operating room. Lying there, thinking and feeling the fear of contracting COVID-19 while also feeling increasingly claustrophobic and suffocated because of the mask.

This surgery forced me to take time off, be open and honest with clients about boundaries, and rely on my team. And you know what? They were all there for me. The ankle break had shown me the depth of love I had around me and that my identity was not solely defined by work. The last surgery taught me the importance of prioritizing my well-being and elevating self-care—a lesson I had yet to fully grasp and still need to practice daily.

Throughout this process, I learned so much. I discovered how to be present with myself and embrace stillness. I realized I had the strength to remain calm, waiting patiently for my husband for 40 minutes. I learned to keep my composure during the car ride to the emergency room and endure X-rays without pain medication. I discovered the power of accepting help and experiencing unconditional love. For weeks, I had nothing to offer—no job, no entertaining conversations. Nothing. Yet, my friends and family stood by me. I also learned the depths of my love for my husband and the depth of his love for me.

I learned how to be a better friend – how to care and support others. I had never been good at reaching out to others in general, let alone during their times of need. But now I understood the impact a simple phone call, email, or text could have. Seriously, a quick "How ya doin'?" made such a difference.

I learned to appreciate the things I had taken for granted. Five weeks into my recovery, my friend Audrey visited from Seattle. She helped me to the car, and I drove us to get our nails done (thank goodness it was my left ankle). It took twice as long, but we managed. We went for massages, ate at our favorite spots, and even the Holy Grail, a trip to Target. Proudly flying down the aisles in a scooter, I experienced the kindness of strangers cheering me on, carrying bags, and holding doors.

Through all my experiences, that one sage piece of advice held true: there's no bypassing our emotions. We must navigate through them to emerge on the other side—focused, at peace with ourselves, and grateful for our human experience.

I'm not particularly religious, but I'm open to the idea that there's a higher power—an almighty being, whether it be God, the universe, or energy. I've struggled to find purpose and meaning in life. Why are we here? Is there more to this existence? How can I feel like I've done enough? My belief now centers around viewing the human experience as a gift from this higher power. Our purpose is to do good in the world and embrace the full spectrum of emotions. We shouldn't numb the pain but rather fully immerse ourselves in it—loving, hating, pushing through, and learning from it. However, we can only do this with the support of a community and with love and kindness toward one another, not alone.

Something you should know about me is that I always follow through. When I make a promise or commitment, I see it through to the end. Therefore, as I promised, this book will be raw and emotional. I'm not an author, so the writing might be choppy and unorthodox—a compilation of stories. Perhaps you'll judge how certain life situations affected me emotionally (maybe you already have, considering it was just an ankle break, right?). Or perhaps you'll recognize that regardless of how you think a situation "should" impact someone, we are all individuals with our own baggage. That is my goal in sharing this story. To connect us with something relatable. Many of you reading this book have either personally experienced breaking a bone or have known someone who has at some point in your life. It's about looking at that experience from a different perspective, offering a new way to relate to it. Seeing the experience through a different lens.

So, let's embrace that understanding and learn how to lean on one another. Learn to show up for each other more. Let's bridge the gap and recognize the importance of feeling comfortable, understanding that we matter, acknowledging that our feelings matter, appreciating that we each handle grief differently, and learning to ask for help—faster than I did at age 38.

As my favorite Peloton instructor, Robin Arzon, often says, "You are a limited edition. There is nobody else like you."

2

Navigating Adolescence: Growing Into Myself

I understand that revisiting the past, particularly childhood, can sometimes be tedious in books or movies. However, I believe it's important to understand where the cracks in my heart began to form, scars that have healed over many times. These scars have made me resilient, but I still rely on the support of my community. Sharing my story will not only demonstrate the difficult experiences I've endured, but that I truly can appreciate hard times, which helps emphasize the significance of normalizing grief surrounding the loss of our beloved pets. Their passing holds immense meaning for us. I'll keep it brief and move on to the highlights, but we need to delve into those early experiences.

I was born in Austin, Texas to a set of parents who longed for me. They had experienced three miscarriages prior and had fertility treatments to make me possible. Anyone would have believed this would be the start to the all-American family dream. Both my parents were Hispanic, with my father having a better command of English as he worked for Continental Airlines at the time. My mom was pregnant soon after with my sister. Life was moving forward according to plan. However, things took a turn.

I don't have all the details, but I know that my father began an affair with my mother's best friend. At some point, it was revealed, and both women gave him an ultimatum to choose between them. Even today, it shocks and saddens me to think about it, but I understand that different times and circumstances can lead people to make unexpected choices. My father chose the other family. He told us directly, "This is my new family now, but I'll always love you and visit you." It was a harsh blow, leaving me feeling inadequate and unworthy. I had been a daddy's girl.

My mom did her best, but we couldn't make things work, so she decided to move us to Farmington, Missouri, where her brother, a doctor, lived. This move showed me the importance of seeking help and witnessing how others can show up for you. My uncle allowed us to move into his basement until we could get back on our feet. During the first year there, my dad would call and promise to visit us, but something always seemed to come up. He went as far as calling us on Christmas day claiming to be driving to see us and providing updates from rest stops along the way. My sister and I eagerly awaited by the living room window. I fell in love with the way snow falls, watching it for hours. We were watching the road and getting excited whenever we saw headlights approaching; however, each time, we were left disappointed as the lights passed our house. On that Christmas evening, around 10pm, my dad called to say that their car had broken down, and he wouldn't be able to make it. At least, that's the story we were told. In reality, I overheard the conversation when I took a "bathroom break". The phone hung on a wall in the dining room that separated the kitchen from the living room. This wall was by the hallway leading to the bedrooms and bathroom. It was a corded phone, so my mom had to stay nearby. I had a gut feeling that he wouldn't come, and my fears were confirmed.

I stood on the other side of the wall hearing my mom on the phone. "What do you mean you're not coming?" Pause. "Yes, but the girls have been waiting by the window for hours." Pause. A gasp. "Frank you never were coming. Was this all a game to get them excited? This is how you thought you would show them you love them, but not have to come?" I can't remember what was said after that. I felt my whole world darken around me realizing he wasn't coming and from what I could tell, he never was. I cried in the bathroom, pulled myself together, wiped away my tears, and returned to the living room, pretending I hadn't heard anything.

My mom was waiting for me by my sister on the floor and said she had something important to tell us both. She told us our dad's car broke down and he wouldn't be able to visit us. The disappointment and pain of that moment further widened the hole in my heart. It felt like the edges of that hole were eroding, crumbling away like rocks and sand in a sinkhole. A few months later, I had a private conversation with my mom, and she admitted what had really happened. She shared more details about my dad choosing her best friend. As a single parent in a small town with no friends, she felt the need to confide in me, thinking I was mature enough to handle the information. At the time, I felt special and important, but now I realize it hurt me more than I care to admit because I was not ready to learn those lessons.

It became clear to me that my dad had chosen another family, another daughter and even had another baby, and they were a better option than us. I can't describe how that felt other than shame and self-doubt, wondering what is wrong me that he wouldn't choose me.

Before moving to Farmington, my sister and I started taking English classes. In Texas, it was possible to get by without speaking English, as there was a large Hispanic population where Spanish sufficed both at school and work. However, my mom knew that in Farmington, MO we had to learn English to fit in. I vividly remember sitting in a classroom, pointing at images while the teacher taught me basic English vocabulary. I was stubborn. The teacher would say "This is a shoe" and my reply "No, that is a zapato". My mom had a black box filled with cassette tapes on how to speak English, and we would listen and practice together. She wanted me to fit in so badly. Eventually, I mastered the language and shed my accent.

My sister ended up in serious speech classes because she just wouldn't speak much for a good two years. They say younger siblings tend to rely on their older siblings to communicate, and that may have played a part, but now I understand it may have also been her way of coping. While I may talk my feelings out, my sister keeps them in and shuts down. I used to believe she had a special gift of being able to cut things completely out of her life and not look back. As I've grown and learned more about life, I've realized the importance of working through our grief and sadness and seeking support from others.

My mom found a job as an office manager at my aunt's workplace. She began earning her own income and even started going line dancing. I was proud of her. We would watch her dress up in her cowboy boots, flowing skirt, big earrings, and signature red lipstick. She would head to the local country bar, coming home late and smelling of smoke. It seemed to make her happy. Meanwhile, my sister and I kept ourselves occupied, playing with our cousins and adapting to our new life. My mom started dating. She met someone, and it became serious. I don't really recall the courtship, but we ended up moving out of my uncle's basement and in with her boyfriend. This would be the start of a few moves and new boyfriends. I really do believe she was trying her best. I do not fault her for trying to figure it out. Most boyfriends were harmless. Some were aggravated by kids, and others we got really attached to, so when it was over, the heartbreak was real for all three of us.

After a few years, my mom shared the good news that we would be getting our own place. Each of us would have our own bedroom. We moved into a long green trailer in a small one road trailer park. Living there was challenging, as it was never warm enough and it was infested with ants. I remember ants sometimes falling from my hair while at school. However, it was closer to the grocery store, allowing us to walk there when our food stamps arrived in the mail.

We would divide the stamps and prepare for our store visit. Food stamps are better now, and on cards that look like credit cards, but at the time they were actual stamps, like a coupon book. Each stamp had an image of what we could have and then instructions to find the one on the shelf that had "WIC" on the label. The labels were easy to spot because they were bright yellow. The stamps always included the essentials; milk, butter, bread, boxed mashed potatoes (they last so much longer than real potatoes), but we always had two for Hostess cakes! It was such a delight to stand in that aisle and really think about which ones we wanted. That feeling went away when we would get to the cashier. As she would scan each item, we would flip our stamp book to tear out the appropriate stamp. It took sooo long. We tried to go later in the night when we wouldn't see anyone there or have many people in line, but someone always was, and you could tell they were annoyed with how long it took. We could feel their stares in the back of our heads.

My mom eventually moved us to an apartment of our own, and while it was all the way across town away from stores, it was our little safe haven. It was warm, it looked newer, and it was ours. She still would get dressed up and go out. She only brought a man home one time, and we didn't even really see him. It was more of a shadow going past our bedroom into hers and he was gone before morning. She did have a longer relationship while we were there. David. We fell in love with David. To this day I'm not sure what happened, but that relationship ended abruptly.

We did have great memories in that apartment. We hosted birthday parties where 25 of my friends would come over and all squeeze ourselves into that little space. It felt good not to be embarrassed or worried about ants. They all also showed up for me with no judgment. That apartment also had a memory that took years of therapy for me to work through. This experience I debated sharing in this book because of how vulnerable I would need to be, but I think it's important to share for all the reasons I said at the beginning of this book. I won't be going into much detail, but you'll understand how my sink hole within my heart grew bigger. I survived an instance of sexual abuse at 12. I shared with my mom, who shared with the rest of the family, and we discovered that I wasn't the only one in our family it happened to. You must remember different families have different ways to cope. The coping mechanisms come not only from cultural influences, but also how family members themselves were raised. The family decision at the time was that it was best to put me in therapy, they would just ensure he was never alone with anyone again. Given that my abuser didn't live in Missouri, but in Texas where the others who had also survived it lived, they felt I would be safe.

It was a hard experience to know that I was believed, but I wasn't important enough to do more than that. As an adult now, thinking of the earth I would scorch if anything like that ever happened to my nephews, it's truly mindboggling. I know times were different then and I also recognize that adults are only children grown up. I know now they have only the same communication, support, and resources to draw upon from their own childhood and how they were brought up. I truly believe each generation is an opportunity to advance, break cycles, and grow.

My mom was getting herself on her feet. I remember the day she told us we were getting a house. That we were able to get the FHA home loan. An FHA loan is a government-backed mortgage loan that can allow you to buy a home with looser financial requirements. You may qualify for an FHA loan if you have debt or a lower credit score. I remember staying at a friend's house and talking about it. I was so excited to have a yard and emotionally excited to start fresh and get out of that apartment. Her dad stopped us in the middle of the conversation sitting at their kitchen table in shock that a 13-year-old even knew what an FHA loan was.

The day we moved into that house was magical. It felt like a fresh start. That house had so many memories, some I care to forget, and others that were really good. I got my Mutly (my first dog) while living in that house. I remember going to Walmart and there was someone sitting outside the door with a box of puppies just giving them away. At the time, that is a real thing that was a normal occurrence in our small town. For whatever reason, I decided to stop and play with them. Mutly looked at me in a way I'll always remember. I held her close and took her home. I worked two jobs to pay for her food, vet bills, and toys when I could. She was mine and I was her mom entrusted to take care of her. That little girl stayed with me for 19 years. She saw me through so much of my life. I needed her.

That's also when my mom had the first boyfriend who stayed for longer than a few months, and actually stayed. His name was Karl. He was a tall black man with a big welcoming smile, who also had the best laugh. I loved Karl. At some point their relationship started to crumble. My mom's health was deteriorating, and she was becoming more reliant on him. Her polio had come back, she was in a lot of pain and on a lot of pain medication. She was in and out of the hospital with lots of doctors' visits. There were days she just wouldn't get out of bed. On her nightstand were rows of orange bottles. Later in life one of my aunts said to me off hand and casually, "there were days I would stop by your house and think we would find your mom dead in her bed from all the opioids." This had not occurred to me back then, and I remember how much it stung the day she said it to me. Now as an adult I wonder, "well, why the hell did you all not do or say something?"

My mom's relationship with Karl ended after a few hard fights, with the worst being when she was helping a friend out and put my car title as collateral for a loan, then her friend didn't pay her back. I remember that week. I was scared they would come take my car at any time. My car that got me to work and to school. At night I would wake up and check out my window to make sure it was still there. My mom had her Nissan Tracker my uncle had given her, and she bought me my car on my birthday by placing it on two credit cards. We were working to pay it off and were so close by this point. I couldn't believe this was happening. The day the loan was due the friend gave her part of the money she owed, Karl gave more from his paycheck, and I had some from my jobs to pay it off. I got to keep my car. I took the title and carried it with me from that day on which I've since learned you shouldn't do that. It should be in a safe, at home.

We went a good eight months without anyone. It was hard. I think I had worked at almost every establishment in that town, held car washes in my neighborhood, and cut grass to make money to help pay for things we needed like bills and things at school. I wanted to fit in so badly. I think I did a good job at it. I made the dance team and was able to pay for my required uniform and shoes. I remember getting out of school by 3pm, heading to dance practice in the gymnasium, being done by 4, and rushing home to catch as much as I could of Oprah before heading to my work shifts that were usually 5-9pm. I truly believe the morals and values I have today are from Oprah and country music.

We were making it through life. Day by day we were getting by. My mom was still sick and not really around much to parent. This led to a lot of poor decisions at parties I attended and boys I dated. It used to hurt to think about how much I craved and needed attention from men in order to feel valued, pretty, and worthy. Not a great thing to be motivated by in high school and also not great situations to end up in. Still, we were making it. By junior year I got a few side jobs at a local gym, Better Bodies. I loved this job. I got to talk to so many people and they used to hold contests. Whoever could sell the most memberships could win a TV. I distinctly remember because I had sold the most and won one of those TVs. I needed it because I had received a speeding ticket the previous week rushing to work after a longer than usual dance practice, so I sold that TV that very day and paid the ticket off. I had been crying and stressed about not knowing how I was going to pay for that ticket. Thinking about not paying and being arrested and going to jail was scary to me. From TV shows, I just knew if I went to jail, I would be beaten up. I had no money to offer gangs to protect me or anyone to come sneak things in for me to "get by". Yes, these are my thoughts and likely the start of my spiral thinking and anxiety.

I had good reason for my anxiety. I had seen the inside of a psychiatric hospital earlier that month and realized all the scenes you see on TV are real. Now I knew I couldn't handle confinement. After Karl left, there was a day I was working one of my shifts and my mom had driven herself to the ER; however, she didn't go to the ER. I'm not actually sure what happened or why, but she drove to the psychiatric hospital in town instead. She made it all the way to the back where they had her in a room preparing to admit her, when she called me. Receiving that call was shocking. I left my shift and headed there. Pulling in, I started thinking about my strategy of how I was going to get her out. I knew I needed to be calm and exude confidence. I walked into the room with three adults sitting at a table. They asked me to sit down and started asking questions. I assured them my mom must have been confused, she really is sick, on a lot of medication, and she goes to the ER a lot. I explained that she and her boyfriend had just broken up. It didn't feel like they were buying it. One of the adults walked out then came back in and sat down. The next line of questioning was more intense. I stood up, slammed my hand on the table and said, "My mom is not crazy. She has no prior visits here, she's on a lot of medications, do we need to get a lawyer? I just need to take her home. Now. This minute." I pulled every word and phrase I could think of from TV shows I had seen. It somehow worked. They brought her up and I drove her home. She didn't have much to say, just sobbed in the car. I thought that was a rock bottom moment. It was a put your head down and put one foot in front of the other moment.

The day I was actually shaken to my core though was not that day. It was on a Saturday where I started my day like I normally do and went into Better Bodies. This shift was only four hours and was focused on calling a list of phone numbers of people who had shown interest in a membership by filling out a piece of paper and putting it into the cardboard box that was at a local restaurant. The goal was trying to get them to come in for a free training session in hopes that it would turn into a membership. I was given this job and the opportunity to sit in the manager's office to make these calls because of my success in winning the TV. I felt like a million bucks that day. I wore a nice professional outfit. I pretended I was the manager and relished sitting in that black leather chair calling up potential clients. I got six appointments made that day. The goal was three, so I was proud. I left feeling on top of the world. I drove home with the windows down. The sun was shining, my country music was playing loudly, and my hair was blowing in the wind.

I pulled into our driveway and waved to our neighbor. I walked inside greeted by my Mutly who, as usual, was so happy to see me. She was jumping around me with her big eyes looking up at me having missed me being gone. It was always such a wonderful feeling coming home to her. I yelled up the stairs "I'm home," and headed to my room to change. The house was so quiet. I felt alone. I walked back into the hallway and peeked in my mom's room. She wasn't there. I looked in the bathroom then headed to the kitchen. Nothing. Everything was in place, but no one was home. I was taken aback because her car was in our driveway. I grabbed some water and was walking towards the living room when I saw the note on the table.

"Mija,

I met a man online. He is my dream man. My friend pick me up and we are going to Texas to meet him. I will call when I get there.

Te amo,

Mom"

My entire world came to a halt. I could feel the blackening in my eyesight starting at my periphery and working its way inward focusing on the note. I read it again. And again. My sister was not home. I sat there with Mutly leaned against me letting it all sink in. Mutly always seemed to know when I needed her most.

When my sister got home, I told her mom had left on a trip for a few days and all would be okay. She was confused, but I was calm, so she went into her room and put on her Ricky Martin CD. I still can't listen to his music because of that day. I sat in my room next to hers for hours completely still and shocked. When would she be back? What if he was a murderer? We didn't have much food in the house, and we didn't have many stamps left. Then problem solving started. McDonald's has the dollar menu. Ramen noodles are ten cents. We would be fine with food. I have a car so we can get there. I didn't feel I had anyone to call, but also, I didn't want to tell anyone either that my mom just left us here. What parent does that? Why are we not a priority like my friends' parents who checked in on them when they stayed elsewhere or who had curfews?

The next day she called. I was angry, but I spoke eerily steadily. "Mom, who are you with? What is his first and last name? I need an address of where you are right now." My priority was getting information police officers could use if something happened. She was laughing and giggling and saying how handsome he was, he had a son who was our age, he really understood her, his apartment was so nice. Then... she passed the phone to him.

> Jeff – "Hiya Erika. I'm Jeff. Don't worry your mom is here and safe with me."
>
> Me – "What is your last name? What is your address?"
>
> Jeff – "Well aren't you straight to the point. Sure. It's..." and he gave me both.
>
> Me – "If you murder my mom, I'll fucking find you. If you hurt her at all.."
>
> Jeff – "Whoa whoa little lady. Your mom and I met in an AOL chatroom, and I can tell you she has my heart. We knew immediately. Don't worry. I love your mom."

My mom got back on the phone. I could feel how hot my face was. I asked when she was coming home. She wasn't sure. She thought she would stay there a week or so. Come back next Sunday and that she would call and check in.

Hanging up the phone, I felt my heart burning in the same way it feels when you have heartburn. That week I took my sister to school, we ate McDonald's and ramen noodles and managed through. I had quit dance by then because of work, but I kept my structure of Oprah and then went to work my night shifts. By Friday I needed to escape my life. I decided to invite all my friends over for a party. My boyfriend was a senior at the time and could somehow get alcohol. I wanted to escape my thoughts, my life, my feelings. Around 30 kids showed up that night. We were drinking in our basement. The alcohol was setting in. Around 10pm bright lights were in the driveway lighting up the full basement. I remember my boyfriend saying, "I think there is a U-haul in your driveway?" I thought I clearly misheard him and then my mom walked in.

She was all smiles, said hello to everyone and said, "Well since you are here, can you all help us unload?" My friends looked at me. I was stunned and in shock. They looked at her, then back at me, and then walked outside to start unloading. My mom walked over to me and said, "Mija Jeff is moving in! He is here with all his things and his son is going to move in too!" I had no words. I watched my friends move their things into the house. I saw Jeff directing them and his son who was a year younger than me and about 300 pounds standing in the driveway, also watching them moving things in. One box at a time out of the truck and into the basement. Each friend coming back and grabbing another one. Once it was all in the house, my friends left without saying much. I stood in the driveway for I'm not really sure how long. I could hear Mutly barking inside. I remembered she and my sister were inside and I ran in. I grabbed them and put them in my room. We slept in my room that night with the door locked and a kitchen knife next to me.

My sister, at fifteen, ended up moving out and into my aunt's house. I could not leave my mom for fear something would happen to her. I slept at night with my door locked, my Mutly, and my knife. I didn't know Jeff or his son. After what happened in the apartment when I was 12, my family (who had the best intentions to protect me) stated they would ensure I would never be alone with my abuser. Despite that, the year prior there was a wedding, and he was there. We were in the same building with everyone. We were heading to the reception hall, and we were all put in different cars to carpool over. I ended up in the backseat of one, and he got in the same car with me on the other side. I could tell he didn't know I was there. My heart stopped and then I felt my uncle open my door, grab my arm, and pull me out of the car.

Remembering this, and knowing anything is possible at any time, I wasn't going to let anything happen to me by a kid who looked like a grown man, nor by a fucking stranger who met a woman online. All I knew was that this stranger had my mom come to visit him, and within seven days, he packed up his entire life and kid, and moved to Farmington, Missouri. I did not feel safe.

Jeff ended up being okay. He took my mom to all her appointments. His son kept to himself in the basement playing video games. People at school would ask me about him, but I just didn't really talk about it. I do believe Jeff is the reason I was able to move out when

I was 18. I had been saving money and buying furniture from Value City and Walmart throughout my senior year with my boyfriend at the time. We had a plan to get out the moment we graduated. We both got jobs in St. Louis and drove the hour and a half up to the city and back for four weeks to make sure they were stable jobs, and that we would be okay to move. I developed a serious need for security and ensuring things were solid. I always made sure we would not just have a plan B, but a plan H, I, J.

The day we moved, my mom was happy, then crying, then happy. It was the first time I really started to see her mental health episodes happening closer together vs the mood swings over a few days. Her comments went from being proud of me to she couldn't believe I was leaving her and saying things you just can't unhear. Jeff was able to calm her as we packed up. I didn't have enough money to pay the required pet deposit for Mutly to live in our apartment in St. Louis, so I had to leave her there for a month. I cried every night without her. I could not stop the thought spiraling wondering if she was okay, was my mom feeding her regularly, was Mutly confused about why I left her? Having a dog is a special bond. You worry about them, and they rely on you to protect them.

I remember the day I got my paycheck that I had budgeted to be able to get her. I went straight to the apartment office to fill out the paperwork, pay the deposit, and drove the 90 min back to Farmington to get her. I grabbed her and turned right around to drive home.

Mutly, my best friend, had transcended the role of a pet and evolved into one of the most profound connections in my life. Through every challenge and obstacle, her eyes held a wisdom that spoke volumes. With her steadfast loyalty, she embraced the role of protector and confidante, embodying an extraordinary bond that words can barely capture.

3

Love and Fate

My high school sweetheart and I got married and spent our 20s trying to navigate adulthood together. We were making it work in our first jobs out of high school. Both of us had opted to work and save before pursuing college. A decision, looking back I sometimes question, as it made for long nights and trips later in my career. During that time, we saved and lived in our little apartment in north St. Louis. He worked at an electronics store, and I got a job at a major hotel chain. Oh, the stories that came out of working there. It was a fast and tiring time, but we saved and bought our first house. It was small, but it was ours. That is also when we added to our family two Labradors, Toby and Bear.

Toby's entrance into my life was a result of a chance encounter with an event held by the Missouri ASPCA. While having no home of his own yet, Toby was the happiest boy. He had a skinny little black body with the longest tail that wiggled so happily. His spirit was tender and kind, almost like a childlike innocence that set him apart from Mutly, who had always emanated a profound wisdom.

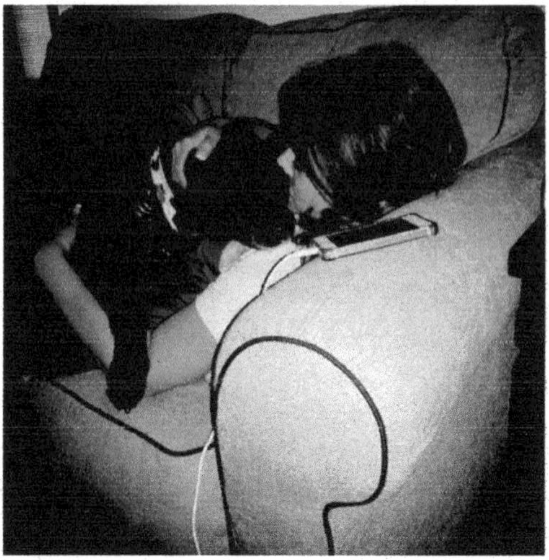

Bear, on the other hand, was a massive 110-pound bundle of affection. Our friend Jessica found herself in the predicament of moving out of state and being unable to take him along. When she reached out on Facebook, an immediate and resolute decision to welcome him into our family was made. Bear had kind eyes and habit of crawling into our laps without realizing his size. I always felt Bear was truly an old soul. He completed our little family.

Marrying your high school sweetheart can be a beautiful journey of growing up in sync, but it can also be challenging as you start to discover and evolve into your adult self. In our case, it felt like one of us was changing from who we used to be. I had bigger dreams and goals than I even knew when we moved out of Farmington. Eventually, we divorced when we were 26.

The aftermath of the divorce sent me into a downward spiral. It was the first time I truly experienced living alone. While I had often felt alone during my upbringing, I still had people around me. But now, it was just me, my faithful companion Mutly, and our new family additions, Toby and Bear.

In the divorce agreement, I got to keep Mutly and Toby, while my ex-husband kept Bear. Since he was waiting to move into an apartment and temporarily living with friends, they stayed with me for the time being. It was a heart-wrenching reality to face that I would only be seeing Mutly and Toby daily soon and not Bear. Determined to cherish every moment, I resolved to spend as much time as possible with Bear until my ex-husband's transition to his new apartment. In a gesture of goodwill, my ex-husband granted me the privilege to visit Bear whenever I missed him. It was during these reflections that I couldn't help but empathize with divorced parents navigating similar circumstances with their human children. The ache of missing out on precious moments and shared memories, along with the fragmentation of the family unit residing under one roof, felt deeply profound.

By this point, I was working as a marketing manager at a pharmaceutical company, traveling to conventions, attending night school to complete my unfinished Bachelor's degree, and simply trying to figure things out. Amidst the chaos, I sometimes overlooked basic tasks, like buying dog food. I vividly remember the day I gave them a loaf of bread as breakfast when I realized I did not have food for them. I discovered this upset their stomachs. It was quite a surprise to come home from work and be greeted by the smell of a mess. I walked into the kitchen, seeing the aftermath, and there they were—looking at me with innocent eyes and wagging tails, overjoyed to see me. Overwhelmed, I leaned against the wall, slid down to the floor, and took in the sight around me.

Another part of the divorce settlement, was selling the house —a process known to be one of the most stressful experiences in life. (It even ranks in the top five on lists you can find with a quick Google search.) This meant having to leave the house every time the realtor informed me of potential buyers coming for a viewing. I would pack the three pups into the car and drive around for an hour, waiting for the coast to clear. One particularly challenging day, I had a work trip scheduled and the basement flooded. It didn't help there was a showing scheduled the next morning. I couldn't afford to skip the trip since my job was essential, so I called my ex-husband to ask for his help. Although he wasn't thrilled, he came and took care of the situation while I went on my trip. Looking back, I wish I had advocated for myself more and asked for more help, but in those days, I was simply surviving day by day.

During this time, I met someone. He made me feel seen, paid attention to, and safe. Although he lived in a different state, we spoke every day, texted hundreds of messages, and even cooked dinner together over FaceTime every single night. Things moved fast, and he started visiting me on weekends, providing a glimmer of hope during my divorce.

He was significantly older than I was and seemed more mature and knowledgeable about running a household and life. With him, I learned practical skills I hadn't grasped while growing up. His concern for my well-being was evident, always wanting to know where I was and who I was with. If I didn't respond to his texts quickly, he'd call multiple times just to ensure I was safe and sound. Coming from a background of no structure, curfews, or rules, his caring nature felt like what love was supposed to feel like —a sense of genuine care and concern from someone who truly wanted to ensure my safety and well-being.

At times, I couldn't help but sense that his caring nature went beyond the ordinary, and others around me noticed it too. There were moments when I felt his intense concern crossed a line, and it made me question the dynamics of our relationship. I remember one incident during a lunch with friends when I accidentally left my phone on silent. Upon returning to my car and checking my phone, I was stunned to find 26 missed calls from him. I immediately called him back, but instead of relief, it ignited a heated argument on the car ride home. The tone of the argument suggested he suspected me of cheating, which left me feeling uneasy.

These moments gave me pause and caused me to reflect on the relationship. Yet, despite these occasional red flags, I couldn't deny the undeniable connection we shared. His unwavering attention and the way he expressed himself with intelligence and eloquence always drew me back. It made me feel cherished and genuinely valued, as if I held a special place in his heart.

After just a few months together, he surprised me with a proposal, and I happily said yes. But there had been conditions tied to my weight. He fell in love with my heart during our long-distance romance, but for the long haul, he wanted me to be in better shape. He noted that being in shape it is a signal to the world that a person "took care of themselves." While we were engaged, he insisted that I couldn't meet his family and friends until I reached the specific goal weight we had agreed upon. We talked about it a lot. I had pushed to at least meet his family when I was withing 15 pounds of the goal, but he told me it would be a fresh start if I just waited to meet everyone as the person I really was and who they would know moving forward. It left me with mixed feelings, wondering what this all really meant.

By this time, I had turned 27, and I agreed with him. I saw the importance of taking care of myself, and he was the first person who showed me this type of attention and care. I had been working out three times a day, restricted my eating to only dinner, and maintained a diet primarily consisting of steak or chicken with two bell peppers cooked in olive oil. The weight was gradually coming off, he visited more frequently, and my friends began to know him. Eventually, he accompanied me back to Farmington to meet my family.

After much discussion, we agreed that once the house sold, I would move to his location. However, we faced a tough decision as he also had a furry companion who was very old and sick. We thought it might be overwhelming to bring both of my mine. It was a difficult time. I had pledged to Toby that I would provide unwavering love and dedicated care. It was agonizing to fathom leaving him behind. How could I reconcile the thought of embarking on this new chapter without him by my side?

As I reflect on those moments, I try to do so without self-judgment, opting instead for a compassionate lens. It's evident now that I was grappling with emotional fragility, which influenced my decision-making. I can now acknowledge that ensuring Toby's well-being and happiness was paramount and I did that. My aunt and uncle graciously offered to take care of him. Although it was emotionally challenging to part ways, knowing Toby was with my family brought a sense of comfort and security. They promised to send me updates and photos often.

I packed up a U-Haul with my belongings, and I enlisted the help of some girlfriends and my friend Chris, whom I had met during night school. Chris was also going through a divorce from his high school sweetheart. We formed a bond as we shared our experiences and supported each other during that difficult time. I appreciated how he knew exactly how I felt.

It only took a few hours to pack up everything, considering my ex-husband had already collected his belongings, and we sold the rest through Facebook and Craigslist. Before hitting the road, we grabbed lunch at Long Horn, and I embarked on the journey eastward with Mutly and a friend who agreed to accompany me and fly back home. It was yet another testament to the fact that friends can become your family and how comforting it feels to be supported.

(Mutly snuggled behind my seat in our U-Haul)

Adjusting to my new life proved to be quite challenging. Everything felt different—the surroundings, the people, and the daily routines. Now, I was spending every day with my fiancé, which was a significant shift from our previous long-distance relationship. As we navigated discussions about living arrangements, routines, and my ongoing weight management, tensions arose and eventually took a darker turn.

During this period, we hastily got married in a backyard ceremony, with only a priest, his mom, and his sister in attendance. It was harder than I imagined changing so much about myself, and only looking to one person for validation. One day, while shopping, we witnessed a mother scolding her daughter in the parking lot. The mother's words triggered a memory for him of a day I had shown some impatience. I hadn't connected the two as I was always on my best behavior and never raised my own voice, but my new husband took it as an opportunity to express disappointment, comparing me to a "terrible mother with no patience for her kids." He suggested that this might affect our intimacy, as he wondered if he would be thinking about whether I'd be a good mother and what if I were to become pregnant. I was taken aback by this conversation, trying to explain that we couldn't judge a situation from a single moment, that raising kids is challenging, and that I didn't agree with how this related to me. But he stood firm in his belief that it revealed something negative about her character (and mine). I was left sitting silently in the passenger seat, trying to comprehend it all as we drove home.

That night was uncomfortable as we sat in silence watching TV. I had my phone in hand and was scrolling through social media. I found myself reminiscing about my life back in Missouri, checking in on my family and friends. He grew upset, claiming that I was "inviting the world into our home" and not being present with him as a family. We tried having a discussion about the link between having social media on my phone and what he meant by it inviting the world into our home, to what being present and loving meant, and back to the incident earlier that day. I struggled to truly understand his perspective.

These discussions were not uncommon for us, and I found them exhausting. More often than not, they would end with my feeling confused and pressured to get on board with his perspective. Occasionally, he would apologize, attributing it to his education. Regarding the experience of seeing the woman in the parking lot, he promised to "not theorize a lack of sexual desire" for me based on something I did or something that reminded him of me. He tried to clarify that he didn't truly mean that I did something wrong; rather, it was his way of "expressing thoughts as a deeply educated man who contemplates everything." He wanted me to appreciate and cherish that aspect of him. He told me I could "cherish that and know that our home would be filled with books and ideas." He encouraged me not to resent it, but rather "embrace the intellectual atmosphere we would share."

Within weeks, it was all over. One evening, I packed up my car with whatever belongings I could fit and grabbed my Mutly. We drove straight to Missouri overnight, with Mutly sleeping soundly in the passenger seat, occasionally waking up to check on me. What a trusted companion she was. I could tell her anything and she was a vault. She had her knowing eyes, but without judgement, she was always there for me.

Mutly was my caretaker. While I got her and was supposed to be her mom, she became my caretaker in my feelings seeing me through high school, moving out, my first divorce, trying to live alone, and now a second divorce. We drove home together down the dark lonely interstate highway.

Back in Missouri, I moved in with friends who graciously allowed me to bring Mutly along. For a little while, I kept my return a secret from my family, feeling a sense of shame. That year was undoubtedly one of the hardest I had ever faced. I felt like I had hit rock bottom. During this time, Mutly emerged as my unwavering support, ensuring I adhered to our daily routines and obligations, even when it seemed insurmountable. Each morning, her bright eyes beckoned me to venture outdoors for our routine potty breaks, serving as a reminder that my responsibilities extended beyond just myself. In doing so, she preserved not only the rhythm of our lives but also safeguarded my own well-being. She became my motivation to embrace the outdoors and embark on walks, a gentle nudge towards self-care that I desperately needed.

Seeking to prove my strength to myself, I decided to sign up for a half marathon. I posted on Facebook about my desire to undertake a challenge, and suggestions poured in—people recommended skydiving, but many leaned toward running.

Chris, my friend who I met in college, helped me move, and had gone through his own divorce, was still in town at that point. He had considered moving to Las Vegas with his friends following his divorce but hadn't decided yet. I managed to convince him to run the race with me. We followed the training schedule together, providing accountability and support. We were both at such low points in our lives that having some structure in the form of the training regimen helped us distract ourselves from the pain. New routines started and I swear every time I laced up my running shoes to meet Chris for our training sessions, Mutly, even at 17 years old, would suddenly burst with full on zoomies around the house. It's like she knew all of this was good for me and wanted to confirm that to me.

As Chris and I got stronger physically, we found ourselves better equipped to handle the challenges life sent our way. Chris had finalized his divorce and I was fortunate to have an excellent attorney who convinced a judge to allow my divorce to be conducted by phone, sparing me the need to fly back.

I got that excellent attorney through my friend Audrey. She was a work colleague turned best friend after I helped her when she went through her divorce a few years back. I had showed up to help her pack up her house and make the move to Seattle. She took me to dinner one night, and during our conversation, she surprised me by offering to pay for my attorney fees. She explained that my support during her difficult time meant a lot to her. I was uncomfortable taking the money, so she asked me to pay it forward someday by helping someone else. Her gift meant everything to me. It was because of her that I did not have to travel back to the east coast.

The day of the divorce arrived, and I found myself sitting in Audrey's office with the phone set to speaker mode, my second husband, and the judge on the line. The proceedings went smoothly, and just as we were about to hang up, we realized the judge was still speaking. To our surprise, he began bad-mouthing my ex-husband, commenting on how he had divorced his wife of many years and moved on to a new relationship that lasted only two weeks. I was surprised at the judgement when again they did not know really anything about our situation. It felt wrong to listen any further, so we quickly ended the call. In that moment, I felt immense relief that the divorce was over, and it was time to move forward in my life.

4

Finding My Soulmate

The next year became a blur as I navigated through life on my own. I found my own apartment and started dating. Chris and I continued to meet for our runs, participating in races not only in St. Louis but also in other cities. We traveled together, always sharing a room but sleeping in separate beds. Sometimes, Chris would stay over at my place, and we would spend the evening talking in my bed, sharing stories from our childhood, and just laughing. He would then head off to sleep on the couch. He would often come to my apartment to do his laundry since I had a washer and dryer. We talked about our dating experiences, both the good and the bad. Over time, we became best friends, spending so much time together. When I had work trips, I would leave Mutly with Chris to watch over her. He would send me photos of them watching baseball games together. Always from behind her head with her big ears watching the tv. She really did watch the games with him. She loved him. He has since shared he needed her as much as I did. She was now **our** little caretaker.

It was much like having a child of my own. Worrying about her health, her food, where she would stay when I traveled, would it be safe there, and my gosh I missed her when I was away. Those photos when I was on trips were everything. There is a very **real** connection between humans and their pets.

Chris became a significant part of my life. More than I think I realized. Later on in our friendship, Chris confessed that he had always been in love with me. Deep down, I had a feeling, but I was so broken at the time that I was afraid of hurting him so refused to admit it. Chris and I shared everything with each other. He was my best friend. During that time, we both underwent significant changes as human beings. We tried new things, discovered who we were as individuals, and determined whom we wanted to become as adults. We needed those changes to grow and stand on our own.

On a normal Saturday, Chris was at my apartment as usual. He had started spending more nights there. I mentioned to him that he was practically always there, so it made more sense for him to stay over instead of driving all the way home when my place was closer to his work. It was simply a matter of convenience and saving gas money. We continued our routine of celebrating a random Tuesday with champagne, enjoying sushi, and having baseball nights or watching TV shows. At the end of the night, he would sleep on the couch while I slept in my bed. Mutly always found her way to check in on him, and then came into my bed.

Eventually, we both came to realize what everyone else already knew—we were in love and couldn't imagine life without each other. Chris knew everything about me, including my baggage, and still loved me. We came out as a couple to our friends, who were not surprised at all. Within a week, Chris moved in with me. It started to feel like our own little family except he knew one piece was missing—Toby. Chris proposed that we reconnect with my aunt and uncle to ask about the possibility of having him back. Though there were no guarantees, as Toby had integrated into their family and routines, they graciously agreed! The day we welcomed Toby back was filled with joy, marking the convergence of four lives within our 910-square-foot apartment. While Chris and Toby didn't form a profound connection, there was a tangible sense of safety for Toby when he nestled in Chris's lap during thunderstorms.

Not too long after Chris moved in, I jokingly mentioned that we should look at engagement rings. To my astonishment, he replied with an enthusiastic, "Okay, lets do it." My jaw dropped, but I quickly recovered, and we headed to Jared's, the Galleria of Jewelry. We started at one end of the engagement ring section and tried on every single ring, laughing, and sharing our opinions. We spent over an hour there, filled with joy.

As we left the store and drove home, I couldn't wipe the smile off my face. That's when Chris casually said, "I would marry you tomorrow if you would say yes." My heart skipped a beat, and I quickly responded, "Me too. So, if you're serious, we should go back and get that ring." It was my way of testing him. Without hesitation, he turned the car around, even though it was in a no U-turn zone.

We bought the ring and were giggling with excitement the entire way back to the apartment. That night, we discussed when to tell our friends and family. It had been only a month since we came out as a couple, but Chris didn't care. He believed it was our life, and we should share the news immediately. He had always consistently and lovingly reinforced the need to speak my mind, be honest, and take action. We sent a photo to our families and made a Facebook post. The comments flooded in with messages like "It's about time!" I couldn't believe it. Our family and friends were genuinely happy for us.

We began planning our wedding while continuing with our lives. I still had to travel for work, but now I had my family waiting for me at home. Chris continued to send me pictures of him, Mutly, and Toby. I missed them so much, but it brought me comfort to know they were safe in our home. Life was good, until it took an unexpected turn. Toby began experiencing issues with his hips, a challenge not uncommon among Labradors, as I learned from our veterinarian. We dedicated ourselves to managing his pain, maintaining a schedule of routine vet visits. However, an incident occurred when Toby injured himself jumping off the bed. We rushed to the vet where he was given a pain-relief injection, and we were informed that age-related hip problems would escalate. Due to his senior age, surgery wasn't advised. We resolved to follow the vet's guidance and focus on pain management. However, just a mere two days later, Toby's discomfort escalated. He was sliding down off the couch not even jumping and he let out the loudest cry. He collapsed to the floor and couldn't manage to get up. Gazing up at us, his once-vibrant face now wore a mask of agony. Chris immediately picked him up and with knowing eyes we were off to the care and to the emergency room, where, once again, we received the same prognosis as our veterinarian had shared. Having rescued Toby we never knew how old he really was. They believed him to be around 11 or 12 and reminded us again this was common in this breed.

It was in that moment, for the first time, that I and Chris were confronted with a weighty decision. We were told it was an act of compassion: to release him from his suffering.

Witnessing his anguish, which had resurfaced mere days after his previous episode and just weeks following the prior one, while also witnessing his weariness and fragility, the very essence of compassion took on a crystalline clarity. With heavy hearts, we held him close as we prepared to say goodbye through euthanasia. He fell asleep in my arms.

In the midst of my tears, I harbored an understanding deep within me that this choice was rooted in compassion. While grief enveloped me, an unshakable conviction resided in my heart — the knowledge that I had given him love and happiness, granting him a joyful existence in this world. I held onto the assurance that I got him back and was the one facilitating his passage to the other side. We lost Toby on a Friday evening. Chris and I were thankful for the weekend ahead, providing us with the time to mourn Toby and hold Mutly tightly. Throughout those days, we held Mutly close, finding comfort in our togetherness. In the face of loss, we were reminded of the need to pause and reflect on the depth of our own existence.

The loss of Toby served as a bitter reminder of Mutly's advancing age. At 19, I couldn't help but wonder about the lifespan of dogs. A quick online search revealed instances of dogs living up to 25 years, and even more astonishingly, a recent article reported a dog who lived to 31 years. However, I tried not to dwell on these numbers, instead focusing on the fact that Mutly had been my devoted companion for so long. She steadfastly stood by me during the most challenging chapters of my life, a constant presence that never wavered. The bond we shared was unparalleled. As I contemplated the idea of a future without her, I recognized that she had already given me everything, and I could never ask for more from her than what she had selflessly gifted.

Chris and I continued with our wedding planning and ultimately made the decision to have a courthouse wedding, and the day was drawing near. Choosing a courthouse wedding brought about some of the most authentic and stress-free moments. Our wedding day unfolded effortlessly, as a chauffeured car transported us to the courthouse. Dressed in his sharp suit and me in a short white dress, we exchanged heartfelt vows, followed by a lovely dinner at a local steakhouse. Our car then returned us to our apartment, which had Mutly greeting us with her tail wagging with excitement. She looked proud.

Once inside, we sent out text messages to close family, and I had already sent out invitations the day before, announcing our elopement and the upcoming celebration in a month's time. It brought a sense of enjoyment to anticipate the reactions of our extended family and friends as they received the news in the coming days. The excitement grew as we received text messages upon the arrival of the invitations. Our choice to get married on an unassuming Tuesday and then commemorate with our loved ones a month later felt absolutely fitting for our unique story.

Mutly became the center of our world. She was the only child with parents who really wanted to spoil her and had time to take her to parks. Amidst the wedding, the establishment of family routines, and work, it felt as if we had captured what the "sweet life" was meant to be.

Then, one day, after returning from a tiring trip, Mutly came and laid on top of me while I took a nap. It was different this time—she curled up on my stomach instead of resting by my side or at my feet. There was something incredibly special about that moment, and I felt the need to cherish it. The room felt heavy, and I knew it was a significant memory that I wanted to hold on to. We slept like that for two hours. Later that day, as we were preparing dinner, I sat on the floor with Mutly and talked to her about my trip and my day, as I had done since I was twelve years old. She got up and moved into a yoga-like pose, stretching her body. Then, she froze. I thought it was so funny. I had never seen her do that. I grabbed my phone and took a Snapchat, sending it to my friends. Just as I hit send, she toppled over and started having a seizure. I screamed, and Chris rushed to my side. Terrified, I looked at him, and he calmly said, "Let's take her to the vet.

We rushed to the emergency room, and by the time we arrived, Mutly appeared fine again, albeit moving slower than usual. We were led to an exam room, where the vet joined us. It was then that we received devastating news—Mutly's body and organs were failing and shutting down. They informed us that they could put her on IVs and eventually send us home with medication, but considering her age of nineteen, they believed she was in pain. They suggested that we seriously consider ending her suffering by making the compassionate decision to let her transition. I sat there unable to say a word. They left the room, and I remained seated there with Chris, holding Mutly in my arms. I looked into her eyes, and she looked tired. She whimpered and buried her head in my chest. I turned to Chris and whispered, "I'm supposed to let her go, aren't I?" I had no idea she had been in pain. How long had she been suffering? How severe was it? She had always been so strong for me.

The vet returned. Chris and I agreed that it was time to let her go. They said they believed it was the right decision. We spent thirty minutes holding and petting Mutly, thanking her for being my lifelong companion and for always keeping me safe. She appeared at ease. The vet returned with the first injection, which relaxed her in my arms. I cradled her like a baby. We were given a few more precious moments before the second injection was administered, and within moments, she peacefully passed away. The room felt empty as the air seemed to leave with her. I found myself in a state of shock. While I had gone through a similar experience with Toby, I hadn't fully comprehended the profound impact it would have on me when Mutly, my steadfast companion of nineteen years, was no longer by my side. The vet asked if we wanted to keep her collar, and without knowing what to say, I simply grabbed it, holding onto her name tag. I was in a daze. I walked slowly to the car, opened the door, got in, closed the door, and then I began to sob.

What had just happened? How could I not have my girl by my side anymore? For nineteen years, she had been with me through every milestone. I don't remember the drive back home. That night, I cried uncontrollably in my bed and somehow eventually fall asleep. I took a vacation day the following day from work but returned the day after. I felt like I was expected to go back. While at work, I found myself alone in a conference room, crying as I called a therapist I had seen when I was going through my divorce. She reassured me that this was a difficult time, that pets hold a significant place in our lives, and losing them can be even more painful than losing a human loved one.

Her validation meant everything to me. I found myself carving out moments at work, retreating to a conference room to let tears flow or slipping away for early lunches to simply catch my breath. Throughout this challenging time, Chris stood as my unwavering support. He shared in the love for Mutly, and together, we navigated the uncharted territory of life without her.

After witnessing my high school days, Jeff moving in, me moving out, two divorces, and now seeing that I was exactly where I was supposed to be, I believe she could finally let go. I had a rock made with Mutly's name on it. I cried a lot that year. Even years later, tears still flow when I talk about her.

My connection with her was a realm apart from that which I shared with Bear or Toby. She transcended the role of a mere pet; she was, without a doubt, my dearest friend. Amidst all the trials life had presented, nothing had rattled me to the core quite like her departure. The intense sorrow that consumed me was an experience entirely unparalleled. I am indebted for the 19 years she graced me with – for her unwavering devotion, her unwavering presence through every circumstance and challenge. She offered a love that was free of judgment, a love that ran immeasurably deep.

Dear Mutly,
I love you. My love for you remains unwavering – from back then, through today, and for all the tomorrows. I hope you're looking down on me with pride.
Love,
Erika

The apartment was quiet, and the emptiness was unmistakable. I had grown up with a loyal canine companion since I was twelve years old, and now, after losing my beloved Mutly, the void seemed overwhelming. Even in the honeymoon stage of our marriage, I yearned for the comforting presence of a four-legged family member to snuggle me to sleep at night. How does one get over such a profound loss? The truth is, I'm still not over it, but in that moment, I thought maybe distracting myself would be a good start. Perhaps a puppy could fill the void?

Chris, who had never been much of a dog guy, also felt the void left by Mutly's absence. The walks we took together, the shared mealtimes, her habit of leaning against us while we watched TV, the comforting weight of her presence between our legs as we slept – these were all part of our daily rhythm. Despite being married to our best friend, a profound sense of emptiness lingered within both of us.

Chris was surprisingly receptive to the idea of bringing a puppy into our lives. We shared a unique understanding that this new furry addition would hold a distinct place. With my life on a stable course and my heart at peace, the role of a caretaker had transformed. I was prepared to channel all my affection and devotion into ensuring this puppy's utmost happiness. We were ready to pour all our love and attention into making this puppy the happiest he could be. He would become our first-born child.

With both of us on board, we began the search for our furry son. Where do we start? What breed should we choose? Remembering I got Mutly at Walmart and rescued Bear and Toby I thought we would head to a rescue. However, Chris has always had a more deliberate approach to life. Something I deeply admire about him. He helped us both to take a moment to pause and really think about what kind of puppy would be happiest with the lifestyle we led. He shared since childhood he had always been fascinated by the regal Chinese Shar Pei. I think he saw one on a calendar and then went into research mode. He had talked about their temperament, energy levels, their loyalty, and even their unique wrinkly butts, despite never having seen one in person. It was settled. A Shar Pei it would be.

Kingston Marshall, our little "honeymoon peiby," was born on March 21st, just a week after our wedding on March 14, 2015. We were ecstatic, but there was a long drive ahead of us. Born in Texas, like me, we embarked on a journey to Oklahoma to meet the breeder who kindly agreed to meet us halfway. Pulling into the agreed-upon fast food chain parking lot, we caught sight of three adorable golden nuggets frolicking in the grassy area nearby. The breeder brought all three puppies in case we didn't bond with the one we had chosen through photos. Chris had his heart set on Kingston, though. There was no other option.

When I bent down to pick him up, Kingston barked at me. A puppy! What puppy does that? I hesitated, suggesting we should pick another one, but Chris insisted that this was our son. Grateful that he had agreed to getting a puppy in the first place, I decided not to push the matter. We packed up Kingston and began the journey back home. Every time I stole a glance at him, I found him sitting regally, his head held high, seemingly assessing his new situation. I felt a mix of nerves and anticipation, as if I were in a job interview, waiting for *his* approval.

And approval did not come easily. Kingston didn't cuddle, didn't come when called, and seemed indifferent to treats. He observed everything from his corner, as if silently deciding whether he would be happy with us. It wasn't what I expected. This wasn't how a dog should behave, I thought. But then I discovered that this was exactly how a Shar Pei behaves. Chris had mentioned this before, emphasizing that they are more like cats than dogs, and that trust and love must be earned. I racked my brain thinking about how I was going to get this nugget to trust me. I realized that I needed to give him space and be patient. I couldn't force his affection. And then, after 16 days, Kingston slowly walked over and climbed into my crossed legs, his decision made. Tears welled up in my eyes as I realized that he had chosen me. I did not move for thirty minutes and just sat there catching my tears from landing on his perfect golden little head. The last thing I needed was for his little highness to get wet and decide this was a mistake. He had CHOSEN me. It all made sense now. I finally understood the difference between a puppy's love that is earned and one that is freely given.

In that moment, I became his mom, and he became my son. I knew there was nothing I wouldn't do for him. I knew this relationship would be different. My love for him was different than anything I had felt before. It was first time I allowed myself, or maybe was emotionally ready, to allow another soul into a place in my heart no human or soul had ever been trusted or allowed to be in.

In the weeks and months that followed, I became obsessed with capturing every moment with Kingston. I couldn't stop taking photos of him. It became a problem, as updating my Facebook album with fifteen photos a day seemed a little excessive. I mean, who needs to see fifteen photos of a trip to Home Depot? We took Kingston everywhere a dog was allowed and of course documented all of it.

A friend suggested starting an Instagram account for him, where I could unapologetically share as many photos as I wanted. And so, we did. That's how meeting so many new friends began. We gained followers and fell in love with other accounts, connecting with fellow dog lovers around the world. Our first love was Bently, a Shar Pei from Canada. Our followers became invested in Kingston's journey and would ask about him if I hadn't post for a few days.

Having an Instagram account for Kingston brought unexpected benefits. Besides having strangers constantly tell you how handsome your son is, there was more. It provided a sense of community and support. Being parents to a Shar Pei comes with its challenges, as the breed is prone to health issues due to their wrinkles. There is fear of kidney failure, and eye issues; there can be specific food you have to give them and special vitamins; and they can have what is called familial Shar Pei Fever (fSPF). It was a lot — so much more than I had ever seen for a dog before. Through Instagram, we met other Shar Pei families who shared similar experiences. We all leaned on each other for tips, advice vets had given, new protocols Dr. Tintle (a world-renowned thought leader dedicated to Shar Pei who has a partnership with Cornell University to continue research on how to help them), and honestly sometimes just a shoulder to cry on when you felt helpless. Those direct messages and comments led to real relationships with families all over the world.

One of the biggest challenges we faced early on was how to care for Kingston when we were at work. Initially, crating him seemed like the reasonable option, considering he was just a puppy, we wanted him to be safe. We also wanted to avoid any messes in the apartment. I had always heard a dog won't go to the bathroom in their crate. But Kingston shattered that assumption. Every day, we would return home to find a complete disaster. He had made it clear that he was unhappy with the arrangement by going to the bathroom in his crate and even rolling around in it to ensure we had more to clean up.

Clearly, a change was needed. We lived in a tiny apartment at the time, so we decided to put up a baby gate and confine him to the kitchen. We got a camera to keep an eye on him, reassuring ourselves that he was okay. Thinking we had solved the problem and feeling quite happy with ourselves I was excited to check the kitchen camera that next day at work. Little did we know the challenges that lay ahead. Our first check in was around 8 a.m., and he was barking and pulling at the gate. Sure - I mean, we just left. He will calm down. 10 a.m. - no change. Okay, that is surprising. Well, I thought, he will tire himself out soon for sure. Every single time I checked that camera he was barking and biting the gate. He literally barked nonstop for seven straight hours. I cannot believe we weren't kicked out of our apartment.

Desperate for a solution, we reached out to our Instagram community, and that's when we learned something remarkable about Shar Pei.

They have an inherent need to feel in control of their environment. They are natural patrollers and guards, constantly on the lookout. It's in their DNA. They need to do their rounds and look out all the windows. They even called it "Pei Patrol". We were shocked. The answer could not possibly be just give him free reign. He already goes to the bathroom in his crate and who knows what destruction he could cause? We were assured that is all he needed and to not be worried about his going in the house anymore. Because "obviously Shar Pei are born potty trained." We were in disbelief, but we decided to trust this community. So, we childproofed the apartment as best we could and left for work, filled with anxiety. Before leaving, I glanced at Kingston, hoping that this newfound freedom would bring him happiness. He sat regally on the couch, seemingly saying, "It's about time." I moved the camera to the living room to keep an eye on him. Throughout the day, we checked in, and to our surprise, there was no barking. He moved from room to room, patrolling his domain. When we returned home, there were no messes, only a wiggly-tailed Kingston. They were right! All he needed was to feel in control, and the apartment became his territory. We kept watching him over the next several days which lead us to a new problem that no wise words would be able to solve. He just looked lonely. I told Chris, and while he was not excited about the prospect of having two dogs in a 900-square-foot apartment, he did not shut down the idea.

Something you have to know about how Chris and I communicate is that it is not always as straight-forward as people might think. There is sort of a scale we, maybe more I, have come up with. When asked a question, if he gives an emphatic NO, with that look in his eye, it is a no. However, when he just says no with no other commentary, well that, my friends, is a maybe. And a maybe is for sure a yes in my book. An "I don't know" or "I'm not sure" is also a yes. And a yes is a yes. So, with his being lukewarm on getting another puppy, in my mind that is basically like his asking for one himself. So, I started the search.

Enter the Mocha Mishka. Kingston was and will always be our first love, but Mishka is our baby girl. Meeting her, however, was heart-breaking and a stark contrast to what we experienced with Kingston. This was a learning experience that not all breeders are equal, and you need to do your research.

We packed up Kingston and drove eight hours to Tennessee excited to meet his sister.

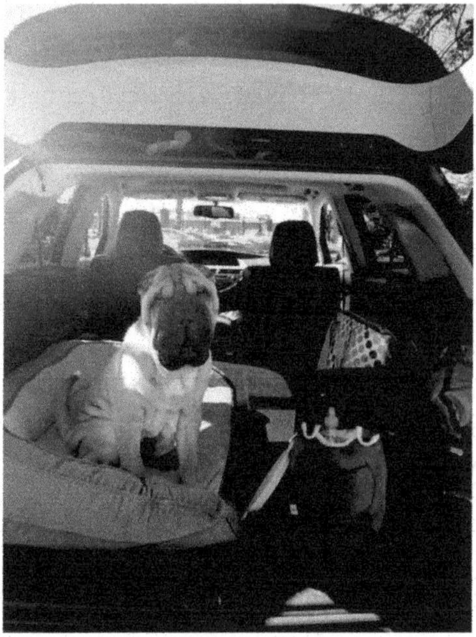

When we pulled up to the place it was hot, loud, and smelled of fresh asphalt, which made it hard to breathe. We were not invited in and asked to wait at the opening of a dark garage where we realized the breeder did not specialize in Shar Pei, but bred many "exotic" animals. They were stacked in cages on top of each other. Mishka was brought out as the "last puppy available" and placed on the ground. She looked up with pleading eyes to take her home. I immediately grabbed her. She had green goop in her nose, eyes, and smelled terribly. Chris and I looked at each other knowing we did not want to support this breeder, but also knowing we could not leave her. Even though the smell of asphalt coming off her filled the SUV, Kingston was in love. Licking, cleaning, and cuddling her. She also clung to him.

We believe she was younger than stated when she ended up in the ICU two days later. She even had to be left in an oxygen chamber over the first weekend we had her. We were asked if we were sure we wanted to go down this financial path since we had only had her two days. Without question, we said yes. While Kingston's love was a slow burn, Mishka came from a different environment. Kingston's first eight weeks of life were spent with a loving family. All Mishka knew was a cage that was kept in the dark surrounded by strange noises. She clung to us and Kingston, obviously never having felt love before. She even more so clung to Chris. It was as if she felt safe with him. His deep voice I think too made her feel she was untouchable in his arms. A true daddy's girl. She immediately stole our hearts, and we loved her fiercely.

She is our fever, itchy skin, allergic, strangely aggressive with sounds peiby. She has taught us that intricate world that sometimes comes with Shar Pei, but she's also daddy's little girl, our Mocha Mishka, and the princess of the house. She is picky with whom she loves, whom she comes close to, and whom she gives her wonderful most perfect delicate sweet-and-not-wet kisses to. She is the first one up, can go zero to 60 in seconds, and has a heart-melting love for wet towels. She is the most wonderful little girl that has grown our hearts in ways we couldn't have imagined. [The breeder no longer breeds dogs. We reported them.]

Now that we were a pack, we walked them every day and took them to a dog park so they could run. We loved our little family. We decided we needed to get them a yard and a house so they could run and have zoomies inside. We really wanted more out of life, but only so we could give it to them. That is love.

(Kingston and Mishka enjoying their favorite park and having a "yard")

We started house hunting and found what could only be described as the American dream house. It was only thirty minutes from where we lived and was perfect for our little family.

The day before we were set to close on the house was the same day I was sat down at my job and told "all the talent is in New Jersey," and that they were closing down the St. Louis offices. Some of us would be given packages as severance, and others would be offered jobs if willing to move. I was offered to be moved. I came home in tears. I didn't want to move to New Jersey. I loved the Midwest, I loved this house, and I loved the space I was going to give to my kids – space I was not going to get in New Jersey. Chris and I talked, and he told me he believed in us and that we needed to bet on ourselves. So, with our immediate future in some serious risk, we closed on our house the next day.

Through some tough conversations at work, I was offered a retention bonus if I was willing to stay on for a year while they found my replacement. When that year finally ended, I didn't want to be extended any longer, even though they tried. I wanted to know where my future was going. I took another risk and let them know they could let me go that day and pay my severance and I would be willing to start Monday as a contractor.

It took some discussions with my former employer, but we made it happen. That single decision opened me up to be a free agent. I now could contract with other companies as a marketer. I wasn't sure how long this gig would last so I took every contract that came my way. It was a hard and fast two years for us. I eventually hit a breaking point trying to do too much as an individual and had my first panic attack. It was scary and it was real. It landed me in the ER. I started thinking more about how to structure my life, where I wanted it to go, and what I wanted out of it. This led to deep discussions about family and babies.

That summer there was work, travel, and real conversations. We had raw conversations about what we wanted our life to look like and how we prioritized each other, our dreams, and our work. We realized that human children weren't in the cards for us. While we stand by this decision, it doesn't mean it wasn't emotionally difficult to admit that especially in today's world where the dream life is to be getting married and have kids.

We both dove into our lives. Work was busy, I started fundraising within our community, and picked up a hobby. I decided to learn photography. As you should realize by now, I don't do anything at 50%. I not only learned photography, but started a little business called PETraits by Erika. My tagline was "pets are family" with the concept that pets should be included formally in family photoshoots, but also have their own little mini shoots because why not? It took off. So many shared they had not thought to bring their dog to a family photoshoot, but it made sense once they saw it. That tagline and concept was my first clue to my calling.

Kingston was my perfect little model. Every new studio set-up or camera setting I wanted to try he would be ready to come model for me. There were times I felt he understood English. I put him on chairs, in milk crates, even had him put his paws on a fancy pillow to pose. I remember saying, "oh Kingston, if only your paws were crossed." And there they were. He crossed them. My little hobby took off pretty fast. I was booked most weekends, and even put together an in-home studio. I made a lot of friends, got the opportunity to photograph police officers with their K-9s (and the resulting photos were hung in their municipalities), and even had a local partnership with a treats store in town. If you want to talk about a bond between dogs and their humans, witnessing the bond between two partners was incredible.

(Officer Spies and Tank)

(Officer Hundelt and Fusion)

I think this was the first time my purpose in helping others understand how much pets matter started tugging at my heart to make itself known. Every session, I could feel the love these families had for their pups, and I could see the adoration those pups had for their families. I still photograph now, but as a real hobby vs. jam packing every weekend with sessions.

One very special thing came out of those sessions that fall. During one of my photoshoots, I met a family with Shar Pei! I couldn't believe it. They had three and one was just a puppy.

I was in love, and when she shared their breeder had a current litter on the way, I knew it was a sign. There was only one thing to do. Get another Pei, of course. I unloaded all of this on Chris, and it ended with his saying we could do what would make me happy, which to me was getting a little blue Shar Pei. He shook his head and said he was not sure, which of course means YES!

We called and put our name on the list if there was a blue one. I had seen pictures of the blue ones and couldn't imagine what they would be like in real life. One day the phone rang. They had two puppies, and one was a blue boy. I sent the deposit that day. This was so different than Kingston and Mishka. This time we got to watch him grow and wait in anticipation for our son. We received weekly photos and on Fridays we got videos. Edmond was loved before we ever met. He is the friendliest of the kids. The emotional one that LOVES to cuddle. He cries when he's mad, sleeps between my legs, and is my little shadow never far away. He brings the fun, the zoomies, the crazy to the pack. He is our crazy blue boy.

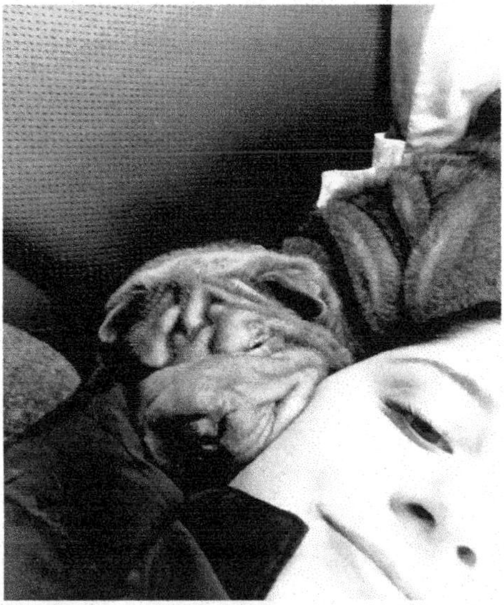

Edmond developed a strong attachment to me, becoming a classic "momma's boy." While Mishka often sought out her dad, I was always accompanied by my boys. They would curl up in my lap, shadow me wherever I went, and display genuine curiosity about whatever I was doing. Our family expanded, and our hearts expanded with it. This period was undeniably special, with the majestic Kingston and the composed Mishka being chased around by an absolute maniac Edmond. The house was never quiet, and it was wonderful.

We also loved the community we were a part of on Instagram. We shared so much with each other and talked almost daily. It got to the point that these people I have never met were some of the most important people in my life. One of us had the idea we should all meet at Barkwells, a dog lovers' resort, in North Carolina.

I don't know how this happened, but we all said yes. We picked a week, and we rented out the entire resort. All the cabins had Shar Pei families in them. We all had to share a cabin with another family. Can you imagine? Sharing a living space with another family and other dogs that you've never met once in real life? Thirty Shar Pei families from across the country packed in their cars all heading to one special place. It was magical. The resort is double fenced so we really could leave all our doors open, and you would have dogs in and out of your cabin. Each morning we would head down to the lake and watch them run free and enjoy each other. Shar Pei aren't usually able to go to dog parks, because other dogs are afraid of their wrinkled faces. Most dogs are not able to tell if Shar Pei is being aggressive or if that's just their face. Yet here they were all the same and they had a BLAST.

With my marketing background, I felt it was only appropriate we invite the local news to come see our National Shar Pei convention. They came and we were on the news that night. It was awesome.

We were so proud of the life we had and the life we were giving our kids. So naturally this is when Edmond decided to start acting out. He wanted more play time, and more attention, and Kingston and Mishka were not having it. Edmond got into everything. We got new couches, which two days later, Edmond destroyed. I remember the day I came home from getting my hair cut to find Edmond in our laundry room, the house dark, and Chris in the shower drinking a scotch. He was so mad at Edmond, but we also couldn't really be mad at him.

I again reached out to our community and asked if anyone had seen this before. All agreed it's the trait of the blue. They are crazy. One of our friends said it was because Kingston and Mishka were paired and older. That we needed a friend for Edmond. I tried to talk to Chris about it and this time I got the bad NO. He said, "If you are having problems with a puppy, you don't fix it with more puppies." I could kind of see his point. So, we sent Edmond to puppy preschool and had no plans of getting a fourth. Strange how life works out.

Shortly after the Barkwells trip, our friend Helen lost her Pei George. It had been some time and the Shar Pei momma's tried convincing her she needed another Pei in her life. She finally agreed! We all jumped into action. Our friend Stephanie from Texas had contacted a breeder in Colorado and found the perfect bear coat Shar Pei pup. Since I had so many airline miles from all my work travel, I was willing to fly her for free as long as I got to tag along. Jenna, another Pei mom who lives in Denver, whom both of us had never met as she had not come to Barkwells, picked us up from the airport and we stayed with her. A true Shar Pei community affair.

The next morning, we woke up like kids on Christmas. At 10am the van showed up. I jumped on Instagram Live to show the world. The door flung open and TWO baby bear coat pei popped out. Everyone freaked. I had hundreds of comments racing down my phone. I kept seeing glimpses of my husband's comments "why are there two", "Did you plan this", "what is happening" etc. I was unfairly being accused of I don't know what. In that moment I was not even considering that I could even have this other puppy. I was there only for Helen to pick up her boy Kirby. All of that fell apart when the breeder said, "Stephanie told me to bring the second one you. Now I told her that's not how this works, but she said to trust her and not to leave until you fell in love." Stephanie had schemed this whole thing to fix our Edmond problem.

Now I was starting to feel like I was in some trouble. I faintly remembered my husband's voice that you don't fix a problem with another puppy or whatever, but all of that went right out the window. I was face-to-face with the most adorable fluffy baby bear and I was willing to risk it all. I was in love. However, after an extremely annoying conversation with the man I happened to be married to where he reminded me that we already have three, that I'm flying back tomorrow, and that we agreed a fourth puppy would send our lives into chaos, I put this living angel back down. We hung up and I sat there. I broke the news to everyone and just tried to be happy for Helen. The breeder stayed just killing time for another thirty minutes when suddenly my phone rang. I looked down. The caller ID read "Husband". "I'm sure he's calling to make sure I'm okay," I told everyone. I answered and without even a "hello," all I hear him say is, "We always wanted a bear..."

I grabbed that little boy, ran into a utility closet, and burst into tears. "REALLY?! OMG. I love him. What will people think? I love him." My absolutely wonderful and handsome husband said it didn't matter what people thought, and he was excited to meet him.

We named him Theodore Benjamin Osgood, aka Teddy. Our little unplanned "Oops" baby. From there it was using those precious airline miles for Teddy's plane ticket, going to PetSmart for a carrier, and bringing him home. Teddy was the missing puzzle piece we didn't know we needed. He is kindness, sunshine, and the warmth of our family. He is every bit as sweet as he looks in his pictures. He is our sweet Teddygrams. I assumed Teddy would develop the closest bond with me, given how the others had naturally gravitated towards their chosen individuals, and I had connected with the boys. However, it was clear that Teddy was Chris's best friend. They shared their own little secret routines, like Chris sharing a Ritz cracker with him in the kitchen when he went to get water before bed each night. Teddy was always the only one who went with him, and well, he was rewarded. Or when we ordered pizza and finished eating, Chris would take the pizza box to the garage, and it was only Teddy who followed him, getting a little bit of crust as a special treat.

Teddy coming home made all the difference with Edmond, too. All of the sudden, it wasn't Kingston and Mishka with Edmond on his own. He had a little brother to play with and together they harassed the other two. So, to this day, whenever someone is having behavior problems with one of their pups my solution is always to get another pup. Ha!

I always joke we work hard for our pups to have a better life. I don't just mean new toys and a big back yard. I mean I want them to have the best care, food, and parents who advocate for their health. I believe there is a pact made when you bring one of these special beings into your life. They will love you unconditionally, the purest love you can find on the planet, but you have to pay that back by trying to be the best parent you can be. They rely on you for food and shelter, but also for you to learn how to give subcutaneous fluids at home if they have frequent fevers. To take them to the vet if their leg swells up, to advocate and push back if everyone is telling you it's just Shar Pei Fever even though you know in your heart it is something else. To have the courage to reach out to the world renowned Shar Pei thought leader, Dr. Tintle, and convince her to consult on a case. To which she correctly identified the swelling as a staph infection and saved Edmond's leg.

These are our children. Pets are part of our family, and we must normalize this fact. Through my own experiences, through all the families we've met through social media, and all the families I met through PETraits by Erika photography, this is not rare. We are not rare.

Being a mom/dad/parent extends far beyond the realm of human children. It encompasses the unconditional love, nurturing, and care we provide to those who rely on us, regardless of species. When you have a pet, you become their parent. You are their source of comfort, their security, and their steadfast companion through all of life's ups and downs. The definition of being a mom transcends biology and encompasses the essence of parenthood — the deep bond formed, the selfless sacrifices made, and the unwavering commitment to their well-being. I hope you've picked up on the parallels between my experiences as a pet parent and the joys and challenges that come with being a human parent. The love, the laughter, the tears, and the growth, all intertwined in a journey of love and family. Being a mom to my kids is a precious role that brings indescribable joy and fulfillment to my life.

PART 3:

CONFRONTING TRAUMA

5

Make Preparations: Facing the Inevitable

We relished in five wonderful years as a family of six. While there were occasional health challenges, overall, it was magical. Every Christmas brought joy as we hung personalized stockings for each of them and watched them play with their new toys on Christmas morning.

They had zoomies every night and we loved watching them play in the yard. There was never a dull moment with always at least two of them conspiring or Kingston taking the lead on house patrols, the others closely trailing behind. Their birthdays were a cause for celebration, marking each passing year. We added an extra layer of joy to these occasions with dog-friendly cakes from Treats Unleashed, a company that wholeheartedly supported my pet photography.

Kingston had a close birthday to my nephew, so we celebrated their birthdays together each year. The year Kingston turned one, Keiden turned eleven. Every year following, we held a themed birthday all the way up to March 2023 when Keiden turned eighteen and Kingston turned eight. It meant everything that Keiden still wanted to share his birthday party with our son, getting their own cakes, presents, and the traditional photo together.

Then, only two months later, the morning of May 16, 2023, Kingston let us know he was not okay. We woke up to hearing him peeing in the house, which he never does. He then slowly walked over to my side of the bed and lied down by the window. His breathing was labored. I got down next to him holding his face and tried to comfort him. Chris stood over us while we looked at him asking him, "Bubby, what's wrong?" While lying there holding him, I started looking at his legs to see if they were swollen, which can be a sign of a fever episode coming on. As I made my way to his back legs, I saw a piece of feces come out.

My leadership and management team flew into St. Louis the day before for a weeklong meeting. Chris, now a stay-at-home dog dad, said, "Babe, this is why we set up our life this way. You head to work; I'll take our son and I'll keep you posted." I eventually agreed and started getting ready. That hour getting ready, my anxiety and worry intensified. I felt something was off. I texted my best friend Yvonne, who has five Shar Pei, lives in San Diego, and is one of the families we met through social media. It was 5am her time, but we as Shar Pei moms have ALWAYS been there for each other: day or night, managing symptoms, and being a shoulder to lean on. She told me she felt I needed to go to the ER with Chris. As we were texting, I was feeling it too.

Chris had made it to the ER parking lot. The ER still had COVID protocols in place where you were instructed to wait in the parking lot and call in. Depending on the type of emergency, they would prioritize when you would come in. When he called, the line intake nurse had said, "So Kingston is eating?" to which he answered, "Yes, he ate dinner last night." She proceeded to, "And he's walking?" and Chris again said, "Yes, but ..." and she interrupted, "And you're here at emergency?" to which he replied, "Yes, something is wrong. I know my son."

Chris said the moment a doctor got in the room and heard Kingston's heart; they immediately took him back. They started prepping an IV. At the same time, I had picked up the phone to call Chris to say I was telling the team I was not coming to them, and that I was on my way to the ER. I felt something was wrong. He answered in tears. He said, "Something is really wrong. They think it's cancer or terminal. They just took him back, but they won't do anything until you get here." I called Yvonne and cried the whole drive there. She kept me calm on that 22-minute drive.

The doctors explained the severity of the situation. They found out he had pericardial effusion. The heart is enclosed with a thin, two-layered membranous sac. Under normal circumstances, a small volume of fluid exists in the space between the two layers. Pericardial effusion refers to the accumulation of fluid – much larger volumes of fluid – in this space. Kingston's was so full.

Pericardial effusion causes compression of the heart, reducing its ability to fill. Cardiac tamponade can occur, causing circulatory collapse. Severely low blood pressure, abnormal heart rhythms (cardiac arrhythmias), and death can follow if not treated.

They took Kingston back to remove the fluid from the pericardial space. This procedure required sedation and advancement of a needle between the ribs into the chest. They said it was risky, but they waited to do it until I arrived so that both Chris and I got to say we loved him and he's a good boy.

Kingston, the strong boy that he is, walked himself out to us almost as if not to worry us. He sat with us and then he got himself up and started walking out of the room like he knew he needed to get back there for relief. That is who Kingston was. He had so much pride. He never wanted us or his siblings to see him hurting. When he would fever from Shar Pei fever, he always left the room. We would have to find him, in contrast to the others, who stay close and want comfort from us when they are not feeling good.

They took Kingston back and started the procedure, then kept him back there until the cardiologist arrived. The cardiologist needed to perform a cardiogram to see if they could see a tumor, as they said this fluid buildup doesn't happen out of nowhere and is usually caused by cancer. The attending veterinarian came back to tell us that we had to wait for cardiologist to do the scan to know anything else. At that moment, as an emergency, they just knew to drain fluids, but told us that "we will be talking days and weeks we have left with him after this." We posted on our socials asking for all love and prayers that we could have more time with Kingston. We asked for prayers for him not to be in pain. At this point, I needed comfort, and I needed a miracle. How best to get one if not by asking 40,000 people to pray for him? We received 200+ comments, and boy, did we feel the power of love around the world.

We got to take him home that day after the fluid drain. The cardiologist did the scan and did not see a tumor, which provided hope. We didn't know how he was okay or what this meant yet. I mean, hours ago, they had just told us to prepare for the worst. They said there was only a 5% chance to get the answer we got that day. That there was no cancer on the scan. They did caveat that it's not to say cancer was not there. It may just be growing or present in the form of mesothelioma. But for now, we just had to watch for fluid buildup symptoms. We would be able to do two more fluid drains, but after that, we would be discussing open heart surgery. They said if there were no more buildups, in a month we would need to bring him back for another echocardiogram to see if a mass could be seen. There was a very small possibility his Shar Pei breed could have caused this swelling that led to the fluid pocket at his heart.

We were so grateful we took him in. They said the fluid pressure buildup on his heart could have caused him to collapse from the heart strain, and he would have had a stroke. They were not sure how long it had been building, so maybe it could have been a long time, which means we may get much more time with him. We got home that night and Mishka was the perfect little nurse by his side.

The next day, May 17, 2023, we posted Kingston has been "okay". Sleepy still, moving slowly, but he was eating. We wished he was flying around with zoomies, but that was too much to ask for at the moment. We shared that we were instructed to come back to see the cardiologist or bring him back in that night if he was lethargic. They also told us he should be feeling so much better having all the fluid drained.

May 18, 2023, Kingston was still moving slowly. We decided to take him back. He was admitted for the day. The fluid had started to come back, his breathing was labored again, and his heart rate was up. This time they drained 110ml from his heart pocket. The cardiologist was to see him again and do another echocardiogram with fluid in sac, which may more clearly show if he has cancer or not. The hope was no cancer, and we truly were the lucky 5% where this just happens to keep reoccurring. If this was the case, they would drain him again. We knew we would have one more drain tap before discussing open heart surgery.

Open heart pericardiectomy is major surgery and is performed via a thoracotomy (opening the chest between the ribs). The great news was that we had one more step (another drain) before this, and even if we ended up needing surgery, it's an 80-90% survival rate longer term. There was so much hope. We kept our followers on socials posted and thanked them for all the prayers, comments, and messages. We read every single one. They meant a lot. We were praying for a miracle for our golden nugget.

The cardiologist came into our room and sat down. She told us the scan clearly showed Kingston did have a tumor on his heart. We started sobbing. She was so kind and told us she knew how hard this was. She asked us to come back the next day to see the oncologist for what we should do next. They let us bring him home.

The next day we had the appointment with the oncologist. We knew it was not going to be great news given they knew he had a tumor, two days prior they drained 70ml, and the day before they drained 110ml. He was more comfortable each time they drained fluid, but only for 18 hours or so. We heard the knock at the door and the oncologist walked in. She explained where the tumor was, how the fluid built up, that this is terminal and aggressive cancer. I asked to see a photo of the scan. I couldn't reconcile looking at my son and knowing there was something wrong that I couldn't see. She opened her laptop and showed us the scan. She let me record her walking us through it and take a photo of the scan.

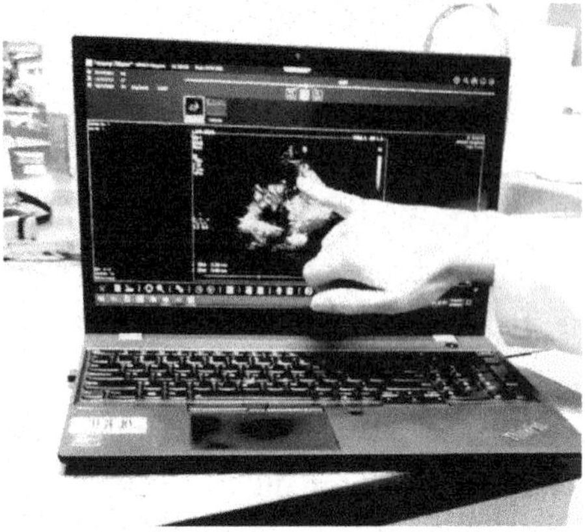

She told us the cancer is so aggressive because it was in his heart. It would spread fast. She added if he didn't have the fluid buildup around his heart, which applies pressure and makes it hard for the heart to beat and for him to breathe, we could have considered chemotherapy and maybe get a week or two more, but it would still be hard on his body and there is no cure. It would only be to try to get more time. Usually with this type of cancer we would get an average of 56 days and they wouldn't be great for Kingston. That this cancer would spread quickly to his belly next and then his lungs, and again, that it would be painful.

We did another scan to see how much fluid was in his heart and were told we could come back that weekend to drain again all in an effort to make him as comfortable as possible until Monday.

Monday, Kingston's vet he's seen his whole life would be coming to our home. Kingston would be in our bed surrounded by his parents and siblings. We knew the biggest gift as parents to him was to end his suffering and pain so he could lay in peace even if it meant that our suffering would begin. We knew this is the burden and responsibility we carry as parents.

I had heard something that stayed with me in the TV show 1883. It was season 1, episode 6. When you love, you trade souls. They get a piece of yours; you get a piece of theirs. So, when they cross over, a little piece of you dies with them. That's why we hurt so badly. But that little piece of them is still inside us, and they can use our eyes to see the world. I held onto this so deeply.

I shared the update to our socials and stated that I was not sure how much I would be able to reply over the next few days, or Monday when it was time. We wanted to be present with him, cuddling him, treating him to his favorite foods. We told our community we planned to post on Monday so they can all pray with us to his ease his transition over that rainbow bridge, but not much activity would follow for a little while as we grieved. We told them we loved them all.

I spent that night hugging my son, reading him the comments from all over the world, and making sure he knew how loved he was. One comment that will forever stay with us:

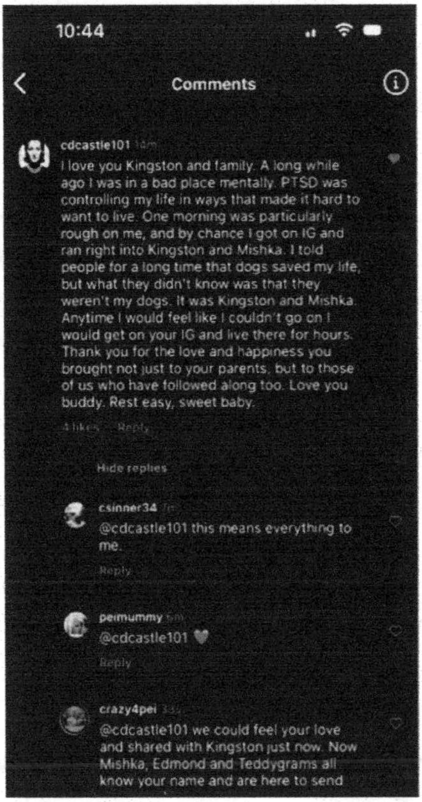

On May 20th, we took Kingston for a walk to Faust Park where we used to take him and Mishka when we lived in our little apartment. I filmed the walk. I then went back and found a video when it was just Kingston as a baby, and he still couldn't beat dad at a race. Then I also found a video when Mishka joined the pack, and they both flew past dad so fast. Today Kingston still had a little trot, but it was hard. I made a compilation video of them and felt compelled to share on our socials. I was getting so many direct messages of prayer and sharing how much they loved him. It felt healing to share with our community who loved him so much that Kingston was enjoying his last days. Making Kingston happy was our top priority. We held back tears knowing we were about to experience the "last" of many of our favorite things, and although he was struggling to walk that day, he was happy being in the fresh air.

That day, I also decided to take pictures of every special part of my golden nugget. It was advice I received from Amy, a fellow Shar Pei mom. I took pictures of his face, his eyes, his tail, his wrinkles on his back legs, his little teeth. Kingston was enjoying his siblings and had enough energy to walk around and sit with them at their windows. These are my most cherished photos now. The look he gave me was an understanding between us both. It was a look he'd never given me before.

I also decided to post that we had been talking to Kingston a lot. Making sure he knows all the things he does that are so funny, sharing memories we love, and how proud we are of him. How many lives he's brought us close to that wouldn't have happened without him. I had also been telling him that soon he's going to be heading to a magical place and make sooo many friends who are already there. I told everyone that I was imagining the smile he had in the video after our park visit the day before is what he'll be doing all day Monday afternoon, but with no pain.

I told our followers that we had been reading every comment. Especially at night when Kingston was sleeping. This was the time I felt I could cry, and he wouldn't know. I shared the thing that made me feel like I could breathe was going back and scrolling through all their comments. Their words truly brought comfort at a time I couldn't seem to calm my heart. Pain came in waves and cut so deeply. I shared that I had made a list for Kingston of ALL his friends who would be waiting to play. I asked our followers if they had a Pei, a pup, a beloved pet who's already playing over that rainbow bridge if they could please comment their name for me to add to my list for him. It brought me comfort to know he was not going to be figuring anything out alone.

279 comments came back with their pet's names on Instagram alone. The comments were more than just their names. They shared how much they still missed their pets, even years later. I diligently wrote each and every name in the notes app on my phone. Honestly, I think doing this was a coping mechanism to do something in those dark nighttime hours, trying to keep it together.

Kingstons friends

Mutley, Bentley, Paige, Jasmine, Topango, Douglas, Murphy, Willow, Einstein, Ruger, Hobbes, George, Thurston, Chuck, Winston, Daisy, Lucky, Dixie, Max, Frank, Marvin, Sparkles, Dexter, Sharmin, Coco, Ike, Gory, Grizz, Lolita, Buddy Bear, Yoger, Aiko, Snausie, Mimi, Frank, Cali, Napa, Roxy, Dio, Gigi, Gronk, Sadie Luv, Boutch, Rosc, Gandalf and Tucker, Abelon, Coco, Nikki your surrogate, Butters, Bentley, Gigi, Roscoe & Boris, Olive, Elyo, Combo, Blue, Holley, Biggs, Lola, Boss, Boshisho, Lou, Tank, Sara Sue, Penny, Chloe, Toby, Mischief, Pie, Chloe, Brooklyn, Mugsey, Dorka, SHadow, Rocky, Lulu, Sasha, Bentley, Daddy, Max, Andrew, Tim, Rickey, Hazel Joy, Lily, Isabella, Munchie, Buddy, Bubba, Tiger, Tigger II, Cosmo, Hooch, Simba, Bashiba, Asia, Bugsy, Keoki, Polo, Khyber, Peanut, Peanut, Nala, Maddie, Delilah, Crinkles, Ralph, Hoffman, Atos, Ollie, Rippie, Omen, Chase, Muffin, Mara, Cotton, Mia, Ruby, Daisy, Bear, Bella, Mushie, Chloe Bear, Wrigley, Bella, Lexi Lu, Buttercup, Layla, Jui, Andra, Ghost, Ling, Suka, Muffin, Sweety, Trotsky, Cleo, Mr Wrinkle, Miss Violet, Grits, Parrish, Spencer, Max, Doogie howler, Akira, Wrinkles, Tutu, Veruca Salt, Jabba, JK Growling, Rudy, Cooper, Wally, Emma, Larry, Lola, Lassie, Duke, Mr Bear, Lily B, Ming Le, Nat-ural, Neo, Kira, Joey, Valentine, Sasha, Chopper, Mia, Kali, Violet, Grits, Parrish, Rocco, Kesha, Butch, Happy, Herbie, Cosmo, Bailey, Finn, Roxy, Muffy, MeiMei, Ali, Chester, Preshus, Bo, Sonny, Silo, Blaze, Bosco, Stella, Keoki, Polo, Maggie, Molly, Helga, Spooky, Lola, Zoe, Dribbles, Elvis, Calvin, Oscar, King, Wiki, Potato, Beth, Chase, Manu, Lucky, Magnus, Bloomer, Gordito, Chubs, Bella, Roxy, Grizzly, Lulo, Guy, Cassie, Ali, Dougal, Annie, Barnabas, Benny, Bayou, Qool, Nikky, Lexi, Spike, Scrappy, Stella, Alvin, Raisin, Max, Julian, Sephora, Orion, Cabot, Sable Mabel & Stella, Nico, Scooter, Timon, Pumbaa & Magnolia, Butkus, Norman-Roomba, Ellie Mae, Otis, Buford, Cash, Princess Zing, Stella, Maiya, Guendolin, Guy, Brodie, Bear, Titus, Lenny, Molly, Passion, Bailey, Giselle, Buca, Effie Trinket, Lolu, Nena, Shelly, Pounce, Saber, Rock, Flurry, Storm, Bootsmann, Sharpie, Orchid, Chuchi, Kadu, Dodo, Lucy, Panda, Big Dog, LingLing, Leila, Brillo, Dimi, Quesa, Sultan, Edgo, Elvis, Max, Tricia, Ginger, Theo, Ferguson, Hersey, Lana, Sugar, Riley, Diki, Kes, Sadie, Cole, Venus, Komsomol, Dollar, Timmy & Seamus, Wheezer, Bruno, Benjamin, Bud and Stella, Snow Pea, Pulga, Oreo, Asia, Pepper, Bobbie, Kayla, Tisbury, George, Falucho, Buffy, Lazarus, Lola, Buba, Hector, Mannie, Lenny, Jackson, Nana, Ally, Wilbur, Obie, Abby, Ollie, Diki, Kell, Changpei, Thor, Suling, Shauhqs, Jazzmin, April, Delta, Indy, Olivia, Lacey, Shelley, Pounce, Saber, Rock, Flurry, Storm, Zeus, Dudley, Jae, Snoopy, Maggie, Baron, Bailey, Baron, Dewey, Jezebel, Chops, Rolo, Wrinkles, Shelley, Lady, Manny, Hans, Bandit, Boomer, Spooky, Riley, Bubba, Shark, Andy, Mexi, Vincent, Sasha, Summer, Snausie, Lucy, Simone, Kimberly, Brodie, Lulu, Jojo, Oliver, Sumo, Theo, Fred, Brutus, Phoebe, Totsie, Minnie, Wilma, Gala, Muffin, Bella, Charlie, Cody, Daisy, Echo, Garth, Maximus, Meeng, Nola, Stella, Travis, Taz, Zeus, Noah, Sadko, Anni, Big Worf, Sam, Zak, Sammy, Josie, Pei Queenie, Sugar, Gigi, Brooklyn, Lilly, Sun, Roxy, Maggie, Mitzi, Ziggy, Tux, Sophie, Casey, Lily, Simba, Ture, Ines, Lola, Spud, Fuji, Recon, Neeko, Simone, Clyde, Diamond, Biddy, Dakota, Malachi, Hobie, Buddy, Abby, Lula, Kiji, Ebbie, Woofie, Tiny Laddie Lady, Curley, Bailey, Ringo, Berto, Bulis, Rick's, Winston, Gory, Bampy, Chikito, Fred, Michimichi, Millie, Leica, Biggieboy, Smolizy, Tonksygirl, Marley, Roo, Effie the Sun Hippo, Ted E Bear, Sachs, Mojo, Patty, Sandy, Peanuts, Paddy, Hot Shot, Kooky, Skippy 2, Honey, Tripper, Peanuts, Murphy, Yoshi, Baggins, Willie, Eva, Konfitsy, Louis, Miss Otis, Miss Daisy, Mr Waller, Sadi, Mr. Rondo, Amelia, Kenzo, Amber, Otis, Bella, Eyal, Louis, Solomon, Lilli, Milli, Dempsey, Niles, Bear & Lillie, Chanel, Moe, Bella Boo, Doni, Akira, Holly and Ninja, Spike, FuManChu, Sumo, Buddha, Lilly, Miso, Roo, Gabby, Buddha, Rambo, Chubby, Blue, Harpo, Mushu, Winston the Aussie chocolate, Ghost, Bear, Oso, Ferdinand Artemis, Ching, Coal, Joey, Bison, Petunia, Bullet, Muttlee rose, Bruiser, Jade, Fibi, Charlie, Beardog, Dixie, Lulu, Leo, Cocopup, Lily, Piggie, Mr Wiggles Evloeg, Turner, AspenTodd, Nyx, Keres & Chewy, Bella, Sampson, Henry, Athena, Goliath, Hannibal, Wally, Frida.

Bob a human who loved Shar Pei. Tommy's Dad. Dad Donald aka Popsmo who loved Shar Pei. Lisa and Lori's dad.

Monday, the day Kingston would be crossing, I would read to him the 100+ friends who would be welcoming him. I also felt some comfort in knowing all those pet owners sent up a prayer for their pup to meet my Kingston with open arms.

There was so much love. There was also opportunity to demonstrate how not to show love even when it's coming from a good place. We received this message.

I replied to her and then decided to scrub the name and post to our stories to share with our followers that even when it comes from a good place, not to send messages like these. This is already an extraordinarily difficult decision, and most of the time you don't know everything that is going on. It was one another indication that helping others understand how to love and support those going through something hard was part of my calling. A nudge in my body leading me to write this book.

I decided it would be healing to share how we would love on Kingston during his last days with us and show the world how they could make their last days with their pup special. We were on a mission to make memories to last a lifetime and to solidify and really feel what our life felt like as a family of four.

On May 21st, we took our kids for ice cream. We loaded them all in the car one last time. First always Teddy, then Mishka, then Kingston who ran around the car first, then Edmond. We were on our way to Sonic. We got them each an ice cream and really took the moment in. I filmed some of it and then found a video of when Edmond was a baby having his first ice cream. We posted a compilation for our followers to see the joy, but also a reminder of what a long, happy eight years we got with Kingston. Driving back, it hit me: that was the last time we would load and unload them into the car. It was hard. We all tried to stay positive for Kingston and just shower him with love.

To try to find comfort, I wanted to feel in control of what was going to happen that next day and make it the best possible experience for our son. I Googled "how to prepare for my dog's euthanasia." Not a lot of great stuff. I decided to call my vet office and ask them, "What will happen that day?" They told me that our veterinarian and the vet tech would leave there at noon so they would arrive at our house by 12:30pm. They would come in and go wherever we felt comfortable. I asked if we should have a sheet or a blanket. They said no, that they would bring everything. They explained that they would arrive in a van, and once they got inside the house, they would walk us through each step. Afterwards, they would take Kingston with them. His ashes would come 1-2 weeks after his passing, if we chose to keep them. I asked how to confirm that we do want his ashes. Would I need to find an urn? She said no, that they have everything that will be needed, and that she would ask the vet tech to bring the book where we could pick it out and also decide if we wanted to do a paw print.

I felt I understood what Monday would be like, so I started searching for a prayer I should say or things I should do. One of our followers had sent beautiful white flowers that arrived Saturday. I put them in the room and they made it smell so beautiful for him. I read that some cultures remove mirrors and open windows, so souls aren't trapped. I wasn't sure I believed it, but it felt good to have something meaningful to do with purpose for him. My friend Mallory, who had been my source of support, had something she wanted to read to him, and I also looked up music I wanted to play to make it peaceful. We wanted Kingston to feel peace and love as he embarked on his journey.

The night before we decided we would order Ruth's Chris that night and get him his own special filet that he would not have to share with his brothers or sister. When it arrived, it was the same barking craze Kingston always led, with the others following close behind. Dad brought the bags into the bedroom, and Kingston jumped on the bed almost knowing there was something special for him. We took him into a separate room from the others to have a moment with just him, Chris and me watching him enjoy his filet. It was beautiful.

We also received advice to record him breathing for a long time and save it in my voice note, so that it would bring comfort to me later. I recorded his snoring, a video of me petting him, and him sleeping on the end of the bed. I have to say these do make me cry. I still can't watch the videos, but I play the sound of him snoring at night sometimes, and it gives me comfort.

That night, we got in bed with full bellies for our sleeps: Edmond as usual between my legs, Mishka between her dad's, Teddy in his bed at the foot of the bed, and Kingston right in between us, leaning against my side. I could feel his labored breathing. I looked around trying to take it all in, knowing this was the last night we would all be going to sleep together like this. The house felt still. Sadness hung in the air. I placed my hand on his soft golden fur. I listened to their snores and their breathing, and eventually closed my eyes.

6

The Day That Changed Everything

Having a date set for Kingston's final moments was difficult. Yet, we knew that providing him a peaceful passing at home was what he deserved. Our trusted veterinarian, who had been a part of Kingston's entire life journey, was there to support us through this heart-wrenching time. We wanted all our children to be present and understand this moment. Their attachment to their big brother was felt; whenever we returned from the ER for a fluid drain without him, they would search the garage, hoping to find him.

Writing about this while the pain is still fresh is challenging, but recounting the days leading up to his passing is important. Those days were a blend of striving to bring him happiness while knowing what lay ahead – a heart-wrenching contrast. The abruptness of his illness caught us off guard; there was no gradual preparation, only an urgent reality. The inability to save him, to rescue him from the clutches of aggressive cancer, haunts me. There was no time to grieve and process. In our conversations, Chris and I realized that even if time had been on our side, it still wouldn't have been enough.

The following provides a detailed account of the day. I've outlined this day alone as it was different from Mutly and Toby. Also, because this book is not meant to be read from start to finish. It is truly meant to be read, based on what you need right now, so, you may not have read Part 1.

For those who are supporting someone about to undergo or facing this experience, it may offer insight into the trauma it entails. To those reading this because you are currently in our position, I hope it helps you in some way to prepare for what lies ahead. And for those who have traversed a similar path, I hope this serves as validation that the experience can indeed be traumatic, without question.

The morning began like any other, with sunlight gently filtering into the room and Kingston peacefully nestled beside me. Chris awoke, and Mishka wagged her tail in the familiar morning routine. However, Kingston, though appearing calm, had a subtle restlessness. He sprang off the bed and made a beeline for his favorite window spot. I drew open the blinds and opened the window, allowing him to fully immerse himself in the sights and sounds of the outside world. "Why haven't I done this for him sooner?" crossed my mind. His joy radiated through his observant gaze at the passing cars, and even a school bus, which he had a fond habit of barking at.

He leaned against me, and together we sat, absorbed in the outside scene. Teddy briefly joined us, while Mishka and Edmond also made their appearances, yet the moment felt uniquely special for us.

Then, Kingston got up and walked to the window in our bedroom. I had already opened those windows to make sure I didn't forget the rituals I wanted to do that day. Kingston settled down, his gaze fixed on our neighbor's yard, much like he had done countless times before. Mishka, Edmond, and Teddy gathered around him, as if absorbing his wisdom. Eventually, he hopped back onto the bed and gazed out of the other window for a while. Then, he made his way to his favorite spot in the living room, where he could overlook the entire house. Teddy joined him, and a sense of tranquility filled the room.

To ensure a calm setting, I crafted a sign to hang on our front door. In bold letters, it conveyed, "Our vet is here right now putting our dog to sleep. Please do not ring the doorbell. We beg of you. If signature required, please take back, and if not, just leave the package." Recognizing the emotional significance of the day, we enlisted extra support to manage logistical aspects. Mallory arrived early that morning and took on the responsibility of attaching the sign to the door. I also reached out to our neighbors, kindly asking them to keep their dogs indoors during the specified time to prevent any excitement or fence-running between our pups.

That morning, we treated ourselves to a special breakfast of pancakes, bacon, and sausage. As the food arrived, all four greeted the delivery man with a chorus of barks, their protective instincts in full display. I tried to absorb it all, understanding that this would soon become a cherished memory. They trailed behind me as I made my way to bed. The breakfast had been ordered with them in mind, and Kingston, in particular, was savoring every bite. I held onto those moments, my eyes glancing at the clock, silently pleading for time to linger. Then, unexpectedly, the doorbell chimed. My heart raced. It was only 11:45am. I cast a quick glance at Chris, mirroring his astonishment. "How can this be?" we both wondered aloud, fully aware that we had until 12:30. Yet, despite our confusion, we welcomed our veterinarian and vet tech into our home.

All the pups barked so much when they walked in. It was chaos instead of peace. We thankfully had Mallory to help corral them. Our veterinarian sat at the bench at the end of our bed and explained to us what was going to happen. First, Kingston would receive a sedative to calm him down, followed by the final injection that would peacefully release him from his suffering. We were told that final injection would work within 10-14 seconds and it would be fast. The pups were still going crazy, and Kingston was growling in response. With some effort, I got him on the bed, and his doctor administered a sedative. I thought it was a "pre" sedative given how much Kingston was worked up.

It took longer than expected for the sedative to take effect. Kingston was restless, making it hard for him to find a comfortable position. I held him close, tears streaming down my face, apologizing for not being able to save him. His heart was beating so fast. I whispered my love for him and reassured him that he was about to embark on a journey where he would be meeting so many new friends.

Our veterinarian's voice held empathy and a shared sense of understanding as he revealed that his own pup had faced the same heart cancer. The conversation shifted to the frustrating reality of treating this particular cancer type, leaving us both feeling a deep sense of powerlessness. The tricky part about this cancer was that it often couldn't be detected until fluid had already infiltrated the heart, leaving little room for effective action. I echoed what the oncologist had told us, emphasizing the complexity of diagnosis, noting that usually the most bloodwork could show is anemia. In Kingston's case, though, his bloodwork had appeared perfectly normal, even on the very day we were seeing the tumor on the scan.

Chris held Teddy back, while Mallory managed Mishka and Edmond. Finally, Kingston settled down next to me, his restlessness still evident despite our close bond. I held him close, embracing him from behind like a baby. Mallory guided the others out of the bedroom, their awareness of the emotional weight in the air apparent. Kingston tried to rise, and with a gentle touch, I guided him back into my arms. I thought our veterinarian would give him another sedative given Kingston was not as calm as Mutly or Toby had been. I just kept whispering how much I love him and trying to take in his smell. I reminded him that he held the role of our firstborn, while Chris cradled his head.

Mallory reentered the room, and then came the pivotal question: "Are you ready for the next one?" We thought it might be another sedative, meant to help him feel less restless. Remembering how things went with Toby and Mutly, I had this idea that the aim was to just make him peaceful and calm. Since Kingston was still unsettled, we thought it would be another calming step. Without fully grasping the weight of the moment, we both answered yes. As the injection entered his system, Kingston's body jerked, then nestled against my arm. We just kept saying his favorite words into his ears, feeling him slip away. The vet placed a stethoscope to his belly and softly confirmed, "Yes, he has passed." Knowing that auditory senses lingered the longest, our tears flowed, comforted by the knowledge that he heard our love until the very end.

Even Mallory later admitted that she wasn't aware the second injection was the final one, or she would have come over to read what she had prepared for Kingston. After he had passed, his veterinarian and the tech left us alone in the room. I clung to Kingston's lifeless body, cradling him like a baby, and crying uncontrollably. I had never felt this burn in my heart before. I pulled his front legs in – like "bunny feet," we called them – and just cradled him. I just kept saying "I'm so sorry Kingston. I'm so sorry. I love you so much. So much." Chris and I sat there just inconsolably sobbing. Eventually, we brought back the others. Teddy hesitated, but Edmond and Mishka hopped onto the bed and took in his scent. We weren't sure if they understood.

The vet returned, gently wrapping Kingston in a blanket before lifting him. As they lifted him, Kingston's head hung low, and fluid trickled from his mouth onto the floor. I couldn't bring myself to let go of him. I walked with them as they made their way towards the front door. They had to navigate around packages that had been delivered that morning. As they walked through the front door, I reached out, touching his lifeless body. His legs dangled from the blanket, and I watched as they disappeared from view. I fell to my knees at the door, the weight of grief crashing over me.

Anguished cries erupted from within me. Chris quietly shut the front door and retreated to our bedroom. I followed, collapsing onto the floor next to one of our chairs. I grabbed a pillow, clutching it tightly against my chest. My cries echoed in the room, a raw outpouring of the agony I felt.

Time seemed to blur. The intensity of my emotions left me thoroughly drained and exhausted. The idea of moving forward without Kingston felt like facing an enormous, empty void that seemed impossible to fill. As moments slipped by, the storm of feelings began to calm, replaced by a heavy quiet that settled around us. Chris and I exchanged a look, a silent understanding of the depth of our shared pain. Our kids came back into the room, their presence a silent show of support for one another. And then, almost as if in response to the collective sadness in the air, fresh tears began to flow.

Initially, I intended to keep the details of that day private. It was a deeply personal and painful experience; one I believed I could never share with anyone. However, it occurred to me that by shedding light on the real, raw aspects of the situation, I might help others grasp the true weight of the trauma we endured. Despite our best efforts to create a calm environment, the sheer intensity of our grief and the unpredictability of the situation left a lasting impact.

7

Coping with Loss

The weight of sadness and pain wasn't just affecting us; it was evident in the way the kids were behaving too. Their energy levels were low, and their usual playful spirits were not as bright as before. They moved around slowly and spent more time sleeping. Mealtime became a challenge as they took turns boycotting their food. We experimented with different food options and feeding times in an attempt to get them to eat. Our vet ended up prescribing a medication to stimulate their appetite.

Then one night, Teddy's breathing took an unusual turn. He was panting, and his mouth was producing an unexpected amount of saliva, which was dripping out. Anxiety gripped me. Chris and I exchanged concerned glances, unsure if this was a serious issue. We wondered whether it could be due to the heat, but his time outside had been limited, and Teddy had been drinking water. We decided that I would take Teddy to the emergency room while Chris stayed home with Mishka and Edmond.

The entire drive was marked by my tears. The route was all too familiar, one I had taken countless times with Kingston in the week prior. Fortunately, the ER wasn't crowded, and every individual there showed kindness. They were fully aware of all that we had just been through with Kingston. They led Teddy and I to the last room down the hallway on the left – the very same room where just days earlier,

I had stood with Kingston, Chris, and the oncologist, absorbing the harsh reality that we had exhausted all viable options.

I sat there on the ground holding Teddy, my body shaking. The veterinarian walked in and quickly reassured me that Teddy's symptoms were just a result of the medication and nothing to worry about. I couldn't help but cry, hugging Teddy tightly, and I found myself apologizing to the her for my emotional response. I explained how it was the same room where we had been with Kingston just days earlier. She was incredibly understanding.

I knew it wasn't deliberate, yet that room's association added to the weight of everything I was experiencing. It seemed like everything was a struggle. Driving Teddy home, the same tears and shaking overtook me once more. It was the same route we had taken with Kingston after every heart drain, ER visit, and oncology appointment in the past week. The trembling seemed to spread through my entire body.

That following week was hard. The house was so quiet. We hadn't realized that Kingston was the instigator of the Pei patrol, so not hearing the familiar sound of paws clicking on the wooden floor as they moved from window to window was a reminder he was gone. When we ordered food and the doorbell rang, there was a quietness that hung in the air. Not a single one of the kids so much as lifted their head or a single ear.

We understood that even amidst our own heartbreak, our kids needed us. We bought toys, experimented with new foods, and stocked up on extra treats, yet nothing seemed to spark their interest. That's when it dawned on us – we needed to infuse joy back into their lives. It wasn't just about them; they needed to witness our excitement as well, to feel a shared sense of happiness. It was about helping them remember what happiness felt like, even if it meant taking small steps at a time. And truthfully, we needed that reminder too.

So, we made a conscious choice to bring some smiles into their lives. It pushed us to take them out, have fun, and show them love. We adapted and beat the Midwest smoldering heat by getting up early and taking them for walks. Seeing us grab our hats and shoes became their cue that walkies were coming. There were moments that took us by surprise. Like when we loaded only three of them into the SUV, skipping Kingston's turn. Our order had always been Teddy, Mishka, Kingston, then Edmond. However, those walks in the fresh air were a relief for all of us. Slowly, their energy returned. Mishka started patrolling again, and Teddy was right behind her. Hearing the house starting to come alive again felt really good. The night Edmond got the zoomies felt like a little miracle. Zoomies were short lived, but still so good to see. They were confused and sad, but they were slowly each coming back to us.

Resuming work the next week presented its own set of challenges. It had been two weeks since the nightmare began, and one week since I lost my Kingston. In my home office, there used to be a cozy corner where Kingston would snuggle on the couch and drop by during the day, now it held an emotional weight of his absence. His usual spot was vacant, a reminder of his presence no longer felt. My eyes would inadvertently land on that empty space, triggering a flood of memories that I couldn't hold back. I remembered his daytime patrols, his visits to my office for a quick hello and a back scratch before heading out again. All those moments I missed so deeply. The days at my desk were short-lived, as grief would overcome me.

If you find yourself preparing for a similar experience or providing support to someone facing it, it's important to recognize that each person's journey is unique. I share our personal experience to offer a glimpse into what might unfold, but I want to stress that no matter how much you prepare, the emotional weight of the moment is beyond anything you can anticipate. Understand that it will be challenging. Build in times for breaks, walks, and not having back-to-back meetings if you can. It's about finding space to breathe.

Also, understand this at the very core of your being: it's undeniably the most significant gift as pet parents to release a pet from pain, even though it signals the start of your own grief. It's the responsibility we shoulder as parents.

Losing Kingston has not only been the hardest experience we've faced as a family, but for me personally. Going through Toby's passing, though incredibly difficult, held a sense of understanding about the natural course of aging. During that time, I still had my caretaker, Mutly, by my side. Losing Toby felt like what may be losing an extended family member may feel like. You love them, you care for them deeply, but as we all age we can understand the cycle of life. Mutly's passing was also an entirely different kind of struggle. She had been a constant for the majority of my life, and her absence was profoundly felt. The transition back to work was tough, and grief still lasts, but the realization I got to love her for 19 years offered comfort. It was also that Mutly really took care of *me*. She was not just a pet; she had been my guardian. Her passing felt more akin to the loss of a healthy parent-adult relationship, with its unique depth and complexity that set it apart from Toby's passing.

Kingston and I had a completely different relationship than I've had with any other soul. I truly believe that every animal has their own unique soul and personality, just as humans do. This individuality is what makes every connection special and truly unique. If you can grasp this concept, then it's simple to understand that, just as in human relationships, there are individuals with whom you share deep connections, as well as those you hold affection for but on a less significant level.

This individuality infuses our bonds with them, making each connection special and one-of-a-kind. As you contemplate these words, you might think about individuals with whom you share deep connections, as well as those you hold affection for but on a less profound level. This realization underpins the essence of this book—it underscores the reality that we cultivate significant relationships, each of which stands as a singular and extraordinary connection.

Kingston wasn't just our son; he was a profound connection that ignited a love I'd never experienced before. His eyes seemed like windows into his soul connecting and seeing me, seemingly understanding every word I spoke. He approached every action thoughtfully, even contemplating trips to the park or entering our room. I hold dear the memories when he'd peer into our bedroom, pausing before deciding to join us or head to his favorite window and how my heart about burst when he made the decision to come cuddle with me in bed. He had thought about it, and in that moment, decided if love and cuddles is what he wanted or if he wanted to patrol. Kingston's routines, carried out like clockwork, from his daily house patrols to his nurturing presence with Mishka, Edmond, and Teddy. He played a significant role in raising each of them – a role that even our online followers recognized through our social media posts. His kindness and affection shone through so brightly. He excelled as a big brother to Mishka, standing as her guardian. With Edmond and Teddy, he acted as a mentor, guiding them in the art of patrolling and gazing out the windows, passing on his wisdom as though sharing his legacy.

Kingston embodied the quintessential big brother and house guardian, filling a distinctive and cherished place within our home. During mornings that I slept in on the weekend, when they all got up to eat breakfast he would run back to bed after they were all finished and jump over and make sure to find my face. We would lock eyes and he would know I was safe then he would continue with his day. He knew when I was having a hard day. He would lean on me as if to say, "I'm here to hold you up momma." He made sure when we slept, even if the others slept on their beds or at our feet, he was snuggled up right next to me on my side or we would sleep back-to-back. His warmth and the feeling of him breathing as I fell asleep was a gentle reassurance. He was always up for anything. The others didn't always want to go places, but Kingston would take long walks with me and never tire. We shared secret "momma and Kingston" days, just the two of us. My love for his soul ran deep.

He also had only just turned 8. We had not experienced grief or loss in this way. The pain was raw and fresh for so long. Each day was a battle, filled with tears and heartache. The grieving process felt like an eternity, with time moving slowly from one second to the next.

We were incredibly fortunate to have an amazing support system that played a crucial role in helping us through this challenging time. Being able to shorten my workdays, take time off, and have others understand the depth of our pain was invaluable. Even during those darkest nights when the grief seemed overwhelming, turning to social media and feeling the love and support from people around the world was everything.

Reflecting on this, we often realize that our journey wouldn't have been manageable without such an exceptional network of compassionate humans, which was also a driving force behind this book. My aim is to raise awareness and foster understanding so that others can experience this kind of unwavering support during their own trying times.

8

Healing in Community: Finding Support and Comfort

I searched for healing everywhere. Our community was our life support. Engaging with others who understood our pain, reading their comments and messages, brought comfort in ways I couldn't have imagined. The text messages and thoughtful gestures from my family and friends were like rays of sunshine during the darkest moments. It felt as if those texts, flowers, wind chimes, and garden stones arrived precisely when I needed them the most.

One particular message from a follower named Rose Ann, deeply resonated with me. She shared her own experience, saying, "I understand, I even took Gabby [ashes] out of the box so I could hold her closer. Sometimes I still grab that box and lose it. I got her back sooner than I thought, and I was getting ready to go away, and they said, 'we can just hold her here.' But I thought, no way is she sitting on a shelf! I'm so happy she's here." Rose Ann's words deeply resonated with me as she genuinely understood the pain I was experiencing and was vulnerable enough to share what some may consider odd. To me though, there was nothing odd about it. I hugged Kingston close when he came home and every now and then kiss his box telling him I love him and miss him.

Throughout this period, she evolved into a close friend. She would touch base every few days, sharing healing quotes and providing a compassionate ear whenever I needed to share my pain or express my frustration at the unfairness of no longer being able to hold Kingston. The incredible thing is that we've never met in person, yet I feel an extraordinary closeness to her. In fact, we're in the process of planning a trip for her to visit us. Feeling seen, understood, and heard by others became everything to me.

Having the support of the community, my friends, family, and even my workplace, was instrumental in my healing journey. They all recognized the depth of my grief and provided unwavering support. I feel incredibly fortunate to have our kids' social media following. Truly having so many who comprehended that our pets are an important part of our family and this was hard.

Moreover, I am grateful to own my own company, which has policies in place for pet bereavement leave. I truly could not have made it through this experience without the support we received and I'm very aware this is not the normal circumstance. This is why I felt a responsibility to share my story, bring awareness to this need, and actual resources to make it happen. While I understand that we can't solve all the world's problems or provide the same level of support to everyone, I believe that by raising awareness and providing resources for change, we can make an impact and it's a start.

Sometimes, all it takes is awareness for us to recognize the validity of our feelings. Acknowledging that the pain and grief we experience is real, is so important. This is the time to reach out to our loved ones, lean on them, and allow ourselves to cry and hurt. It is entirely normal to find it challenging to work or get through the day. That's precisely the mission behind writing this book – to create validation, raise awareness, and build support structures for those who have suffered the loss of a beloved pet.

However, healing takes various forms, and it differs for everyone. In the following, I will explore additional methods that have aided in my healing process, with the hope that one of these approaches may resonate with and help others. Above all, I have learned that being vulnerable enough to ask for help is essential. It is not an easy thing to do, admitting our struggles. But there is compassion in understanding that we are human and that we don't have to know everything. Asking for help and learning to lean on others, including healthcare professionals such as doctors, is a recurring theme in this book I hope you've picked up on.

In our society, we often see a doctor for physical ailments like colds or the flu, or for routine checkups. However, we must recognize that our brain is also a core organ that requires care. Just as we prioritize maintaining good bone health, we need to prioritize our brain health. It takes courage to admit that we are struggling due to our emotions and feelings, and it is something we should all embrace because we deserve to receive support.

I also want to share my therapy experience. While I had been to therapy in the past, this time it was different. I was traumatized by the loss of Kingston, and experienced intrusive thoughts and flashbacks of how unsettled he was and the last jerk he had when he received the final injection. I kept going back to that day. The specific moment would flash in my mind and knock the wind out from me. There were immediate tears, the feeling of not being able to breathe, and it even happened once while driving and I swerved. I could not control when these thoughts would hit me and I knew this more than only the grief.

I tried to contain the memory using the container exercise, a technique I had learned in talk therapy. This exercise starts by taking a moment to get comfortable and then imagining your own container. You spend time thinking about what it looks like, feels like, and even what it is made of. Some people think of a beautiful velvet box in their closet, while others imagine a bank vault under serious lock and key. The idea is that we can let the distress go into the container. We know we can retrieve it any time, but we are just putting it away until we can give it our full attention. When I was in therapy growing up, I placed all my unresolved emotions into a vault. The vault now felt more like a softer box. While I now have the skills to better manage emotions overall, when I reflect on the specific emotions from my formative years, they still bother me, so back in the softer box they go. In contrast, I placed the traumatic memory associated with Kingston's passing in a large vault and threw the key into the metaphoric ocean, thinking my therapist could find the key during our therapy sessions. It wasn't working though. It was still haunting me. I tried to push the traumatic memory away, knowing I would be going to therapy to talk it through, but it was all encompassing and overwhelming.

It was then that I turned to Eye Movement Desensitization and Reprocessing (EMDR) therapy, a technique that focuses on processing traumatic memories by moving the eyes in specific patterns. As described by the Cleveland Clinic, EMDR's goal is to help you heal from trauma or other distressing life experiences. EMDR therapy doesn't require talking in detail about a distressing issue. EMDR instead focuses on changing the emotions, thoughts or behaviors that result from a distressing experience (trauma). This allows your brain to resume a natural healing process. While many people use the words "mind" and "brain" when referring to the same thing, they're actually different. Your brain is an organ of your body. Your mind is the collection of thoughts, memories, beliefs and experiences that make you who you are. The way your mind works relies on the structure of your brain. That structure involves networks of brain cells communicating across many different areas. That's especially the case with sections that involve your memories and senses. That networking makes it faster and easier for those areas to work together. That's why your senses — sights, sounds, smells, tastes and feels — can bring back strong memories.

During normal events, your brain stores memories smoothly. It also networks the memories, so they connect to other things you remember. During disturbing or upsetting events, that networking doesn't happen correctly. The brain can go "offline," and there's a disconnect between what you experience (feel, hear, see) and what your brain stores in memory through language as in your thoughts and memory of the event.

Often, your brain stores traumatic memories in a way that doesn't allow for healthy healing. Trauma is like a wound that your brain hasn't healed. Because it didn't have the chance to heal, your brain didn't receive the message that the danger is over. Newer experiences can link up to earlier trauma experiences and reinforce a negative experience over and over again that disrupts the links between your senses and memories. It also acts as an injury to your mind. And just like your body is sensitive to pain from an injury, your mind has a higher sensitivity to things you saw, heard, smelled or felt during a trauma-related event. This happens not only with events you can remember, but also with suppressed memories. Much like how you learn not to touch a hot stove because it burns your hand, your mind tries to suppress memories to avoid accessing them because they're painful or upsetting. However, the suppression isn't perfect, meaning the "injury" can still cause negative symptoms, emotions and behaviors[2].

The way I understand it is that overstimulating the senses through EMDR and then recalling the memory allows your brain to make the connection with the memory and help bring the correct emotion to allow for processing. In one session, I was able to process the flashback and transform it into a memory. It was now a horrible thing that happened, but my body and brain understood that Kingston was okay now. He is not in pain, and he is safe. I had to share it here because it was that impactful for me. EMDR provided profound healing that, in my opinion, would have taken months, if not years, to achieve through talk therapy alone.

Throughout my healing journey, the immense power of community solidified for me. From the beginning, I emphasized the importance of normalizing pet grief, and we cannot achieve that without openly discussing it. I received a book, *"The Book of Pet Love & Loss,"* by Sara Bader, from Audrey, that contained quotes from remarkable

---

2 Reference: https://my.clevelandclinic.org/health/treatments/22641-emdr-therapy#:~:text=Eye%20movement%20desensitization%20and%20reprocessing%20(EMDR)%20therapy%20is%20a%20mental,or%20other%20distressing%20life%20experiences.

individuals speaking about their experience of losing a pet. These quotes – from people who are generally admired and considered exceptional by the public at large – highlighted the profound impact of losing a pet on our lives. Seeing these individuals be vulnerable and share the impact of losing their animal made me feel this was normal to hurt this badly.

Another book that has provided healing for me is *"Signs: The Secret Language of the Universe,"* by Laura Lynne Jackson. I will go into how this book created a language for Kingston and us, but I have to share that even prior to receiving this book, I experienced what I believed to be signs from Kingston – attempts from him to reach out and let us know that he was okay. These signs manifested as synchronicities, like stumbling upon his name or references to him in unexpected places. These occurrences solidified my conviction in the existence of a higher power, a web of connection that threads through us all, and the presence of universal energy.

I received a text from Yvonne. She mentioned an upcoming trip to visit her sister, a plan that had been set in motion since February. The intriguing part? Her sister resided in KINGSTON, OK. To add to the intrigue, the county in which the town of Kingston is located is Marshall County.

Kingston's full name is Kingston Marshall. What are the chances of that? There were more instances like this unfolding. Chris had golf on TV one day while resting in bed, and I was seated on the floor, sewing one of the dog beds. Unintentionally, he had picked the wrong golf channel – the tournament of champions instead of the PGA channel. Just before he could switch it, the announcer's voice caught my attention, "... and here comes James Kingston for his chance." My ears perked up, and I asked Chris, "Did you catch that?" He shook his head no, but now the name was displayed on the screen. We both lingered in that moment, a silent understanding passing between us.

This leads me to what I want to talk about now: the universe. Earlier in this book, I shared I'm not someone who's particularly religious. But when faced with death, it's like our survival instinct kicks in and we search for any source of comfort we can find. In the past couple of years, I've been opening myself up to the idea of a larger cosmic picture, a higher power. I've started to believe that we're all somehow connected and that there's this kind of energy that we can actually feel. You know how sometimes you walk into a room, and you can just sense the vibes, even if no one's saying a word? There's so much about life that doesn't have a clear explanation. Growing up Catholic, I learned the importance of faith and being receptive to something greater than ourselves. As I've embarked on a more personal exploration of spirituality, I've gradually become more receptive to the idea of mediums.

In the days leading up to Kingston's passing, an unexpected marketing email from celebrity medium appeared in my inbox. Chris had shared a TikTok video featuring this medium a few months earlier, back when he had a TV show as a cab driver. I witnessed how effortlessly he brought closure to his passengers during short cab rides, granting them peace and enabling them to move forward from their pain. The impact of that video was profound, prompting us to binge-watch all his TikTok content that evening. Intrigued, I delved into researching him the next day. I followed him on Instagram and impulsively purchased a reading from him, although I wasn't entirely certain about its purpose at the time.

This medium's reputation spanned the globe, and given his frequent travels, the waitlist for a one-hour Zoom call was dauntingly long—over six months. However, three days prior to Kington's passing. I received an email with a subject line: Mini Reading. The email stated that once paid, I would receive an email to pick a date and time for him to call me. The reading would last 15-20 minutes. All I had to do was reply to that email, and payment instructions would be sent. Immediately, I replied.

Kingston passed on Monday, May 22, 2023. On Tuesday, May 23rd, 2023, around 2pm, Chris and I were lying in bed. (This date – May 23rd – will be important to remember later.) Chris was sleeping, and I was coming in and out of sleep and intermittently crying. My phone rang. "Hi, this is." Call drops. My phone rings again. "Hi, again. Sorry about that, are you ready to…" Call drops again. I receive a text to call him when I have good signal.

I practically punched Chris, startling him awake. I jumped out of bed and headed to the living room, following the cell service bars on my phone. I stopped abruptly in the middle of the living room, where my phone showed three bars. I fell to the floor on the carpet to call him back. Looking back, I was sitting in Kingston's favorite place in our home. I sat there holding Kingston's photo (which I seemed to have grabbed as I ran into the living room) against my heart, saying out loud, almost willing it to be true, "Please work. Please work." I had watched another medium show on TV where prior to a reading, someone wrote on a piece of paper something they wanted their loved one to bring up that no one else knew. They felt that this is how they would know if what the medium was channeling was real. I decided I wanted Kingston to reference the altar we made him that morning, to somehow mention it. Before I could ring the medium, he called me. Chris had gotten up and came to sit next to me.

I don't want to share the full call because it was so special, and I'm choosing to keep it for us. However, every single thing was spot on and there are areas I do want to share. He told us that Kingston wanted us to know nothing was our fault, that it was exactly the right time, and a gift to him to end his suffering. He said that Kingston knew he was passing soon. The medium asked if it was cancer that took him. We confirmed. He continued, mentioning that he sensed the cancer was within his heart. He then mentioned something about a living dog with a leg issue or a small problem with a leg. We said no, completely forgetting that Edmond was scheduled to go for an X-ray that morning for a leg issue. He didn't let it go and came back and said, "this is for a gray dog, like someone that's around you right now". We then realized he was referring to Edmond, who was sitting next to us on the floor. He went back to talking about Kingston, and he brought up the feeling of getting rid of fluid or having fluid back up in his body. I couldn't believe that a celebrity medium, who doesn't know who we are, was mentioning so many accurate details. Even if he went to our social media feeds, he wouldn't have known Edmond was supposed to go in for an X-ray or many other details, including the part that comes next.

He said Kingston was showing him a picture of himself by the water or by a big lake, and he asked us if Kingston liked water. I said no and in fact he hated water. The medium again didn't let it go and said, "okay, well, for some reason it's him in front of water." Then it hit me: the photo. I had grabbed a photo of Kingston to put on his altar, and it was him at Barkwells smiling on the dock in front of water. He also asked if we had Kingston's ashes. We said not yet, given he just passed yesterday, and the medium said that Kingston said it was important to him that we have them. Which, of course, we planned to place his ashes on his altar. My boy was mentioning our altar - and we had not shared that on any social media feeds.

I can't adequately convey the feelings of reassurance that flooded me after that call, especially considering it happened just a day after Kingston's passing. However, the following week proved to be quite a struggle for me. In an effort to connect with the outside world, I headed to a store, but it quickly became overwhelming – the noise, the crowd, everything. I didn't even make it down a single aisle before heading back to the car. Taking a moment to collect myself, I settled in the parking lot, allowing a few minutes to simply breathe. I occupied myself by scrolling through my phone to pass the time. As I checked my email, I was taken aback to find another message from the medium, the subject line the same as before. Without hesitation, I replied.

The second call took place on June 2nd at 8:45 pm. Chris decided to sit this one out. He wanted to hold onto the hope we got from the first call and was worried that if this one didn't go well, he might start doubting whether it was really Kingston. As for me, my heart was just hurting, and I couldn't wait for the call. I was hoping this time it wouldn't be as raw, so I could talk without breaking down in uncontrollable tears. As we started the conversation, the medium grounded himself and began, "Okay, a dog, right?" Then he mentioned, "Kingston's talking about… did a lot of stuff start in January? I don't know why I'm seeing this, but did stuff start going bad at that time?" I was taken aback. What neither the medium nor anyone on our social media knew – only fellow Shar Pei moms close to us – was that in January, all our kids were fevering, one after the other. We were perplexed as Shar Pei fever is not contagious. We took them to the vet, ran comprehensive bloodwork panels, and found nothing. Despite medication adjustments, something felt amiss for a full three weeks during that January.

The medium then continued, "Who likes ice cubes?" – and that was undoubtedly Kingston! He was the only one who had a daily ritual of asking for ice cubes, something we had never shared on social media. He proceeded, "I feel like Kingston's very connected to you, like a deep spiritual connection that is aligned with your work or purpose. Do you think that's true?" It was at that moment I replied, "Yeah. I mean, I feel like I've discovered my life's purpose. I know that sounds crazy. And that was one of the things I hoped that maybe Kingston would just say – like wag his tail to say, yes, I'm on the right track." Almost immediately, the medium remarked, "It is coming across like you want to help people when they lose their animals?" I didn't want to reveal too much, so I simply affirmed his insight, but my jaw was dropped as I had already started writing this book.

He asked if I had a final question. I wanted to know who Kingston was with. His response left me astounded, "Do you know who Frank is?" I was taken aback. My biological father's name is Frank, but he was living. I thought hard about who Frank could be and remembered Kingston had crossed paths with Frank at Barkwells. Frank, the sole non-Shar Pei pup at our Shar Pei convention, had left a lasting impression on me and here he was with Kingston.

For the first time since Kingston's passing, I felt a wave of calm washing over me. It was as though he was close by, a reassuring presence. On that very day, my friend Molly had recommended the Laura Lynne Jackson's book on *SIGNS*, I had mentioned before. The book arrived the day after my conversation with the medium, and I eagerly devoured all its contents, completing it within 18 hours. The book further cemented my belief in the intricate connections that shape our lives and the meaningful signs the universe sends our way.

9

Signs from the Universe: Seeking Connection and Meaning

Before we dive into the following events, I want to acknowledge that they may be perceived as too "woo woo" by some. However, I believe in these occurrences and the profound connections we share beyond our earthly lives. If this pushes the boundaries of your comfort level, I completely understand, and you're welcome to skip this part. I don't want this chapter to disconnect you from our story.

If you're open to exploring this journey with me and embracing the belief that our loved ones can communicate with us in extraordinary ways, then let's continue.

After receiving confirmation from a celebrity medium that Kingston is with Frank, I felt compelled to reach out to Jinny, who is Frank's mom and a fellow Shar Pei mom we met on Instagram who had also gone to Barkwells. Chris expressed concerns about reaching out, considering the three-year gap since we had last connected, and the possibility that she may not believe in mediums.

Nevertheless, I had already read the book *SIGNS* and discovered that by asking the universe with an open heart and mind, one could receive a sign when setting an intention and actively looking for it.

I shared what I had learned from the book with Chris, emphasizing something else the medium's had said. During the call, one thing he mentioned was that Kingston would be visiting Chris more. That Chris hadn't been noticing the signs Kingston had been trying to communicate. I shared the book's guidance on picking a sign and suggested that Chris choose something as our personal connection with Kingston. I wanted Chris to be the one selecting something, so he would truly believe. Chris was open to the idea. He has been supportive of my spiritual journey over the past few years and was the one who introduced me to the idea of mediums, so he agreed. He even went on to say that if this all worked and we received a clear sign I could reach out to Jinny. I eagerly anticipated his choice, as it would become our special symbol.

Surprisingly, he chose a turtle. He wanted Kingston to send him a turtle, not just in the physical sense, but also to appear in his dreams that night. I didn't show it, but I spent most of the day feeling upset, thinking, "A turtle?!?" I had given him a list of more "common" signs from the book: butterflies, dragonflies, clouds—anything but turtles. Yet, there it was, spoken into the universe.

Believing in the possibility, I had faith that it would come true. In preparation, I started thinking about how I would reach out to Jinny. I wanted to be ready when Chris received his signs.

I then went to Facebook. There was a turtle in my feed on a page I don't follow. I showed Chris, but his response was rather uncertain. He questioned, "Is that a tortoise?" I clarified, "No, it's a baby turtle". He sat there and said nothing. Deep down, I sensed that he might not believe it was a sign from Kingston to him, because he didn't personally receive it. Still, I kept drafting the text to Jinny, preparing myself to reach out to her the following day. Then Teddy, who was sitting on our bed, suddenly jumped off and approached Kingston's altar. He fixed his gaze on the wall. It was a moment that struck me deeply. I took a photo. 8:21pm.

Feeling all the feelings, I decided to go back to my note to Jinny. As I typed it, I noticed something perplexing. As I outlined what happened with Kingston, the word "tumor," which I frequently write for work due to being in healthcare, had inexplicably autocorrected to "turtle" this time. It struck me, but I chose not to mention it to Chris at that moment. I had decided to save these signs until he truly believed.

It was now 8:24pm. I went back to Facebook. Oh my God. Three more photos of turtles. I couldn't shake off this nagging feeling though, almost as if I were caught in some algorithmic coincidence. I decided I would still have faith and started researching the symbolic meaning of turtles. I was still in shock, but not *entirely* convinced. As I returned to Facebook, another synchronistic occurrence awaited me there. Another photo of a turtle in my feed. I started to doubt all the turtle signs online as now I had been searching for the meaning of turtles and I know how these algorithms work. Once you start, you get all the ads.

However, as if these synchronicities couldn't get any stranger, I stumbled upon a post from the day after Kingston's passing. I was confused. How and why would an algorithm present me with something from 12 days ago? What made it even more astonishing was that it wasn't just any photo—it happened to be World Turtle Day. I couldn't believe it. I decided to search online for confirmation, and there it was, undeniable evidence. The day following Kingston's passing, the very day when signs from him would be expected, aligned with World Turtle Day. The coincidence seemed too extraordinary to be mere chance. It was now 10:17pm.

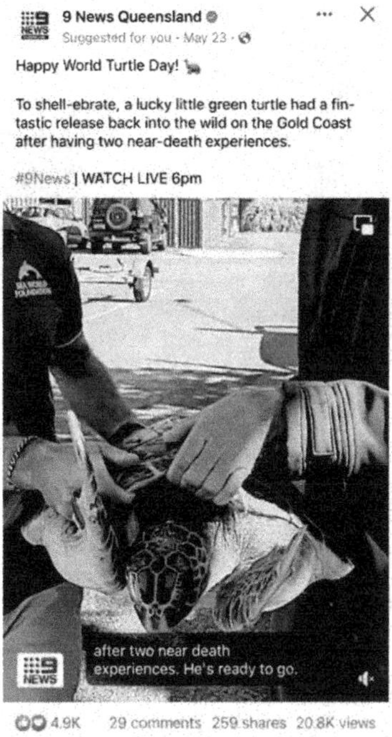

I was left in complete disbelief. How could all of these remarkable occurrences be happening? In my quest for answers, I returned to Facebook, feeling a growing sense that Kingston must have been frustrated with me for not believing. I had to share this one because I was in so much denial internally while still wanting to believe, and then to have received this. It was 10:56pm.

A mixture of laughter and disbelief escaped me as I captured a screenshot of the turtle post. This was beyond the realm of algorithms now. It came from a page I actually followed, known for sharing all sorts of content, and yet here they were, posting about turtles. I still said nothing, and I kept it to myself. Earlier that night, Chris had retreated upstairs to play his favorite video game, Call of Duty. It was his way of escaping reality. I got really emotional that night. I thought through all of my signs, but I was still overcome with grief and missing Kingston. I was also sad Chris had not directly experienced any turtle signs of his own. Would he believe me? Was this truly Kingston communicating with me? Why did I receive the signs when it was Chris who asked for the turtle?

I decided to read more of my *SIGNS* book. Maybe I would discover the exact words to say and confirm the signs. Although it was already midnight, I needed to find comfort and thought it may be within its pages. I read a few more pages and finished the chapter I was on, but my heart burned for a sign beyond my phone. The stories I had read so far involved tangible signs—voicemails, dollar bills with names on them—things you could touch, see, and feel. How would I ever receive a turtle in that way? Exhaustion weighed heavily upon me, my eyes stinging from tears and how late it was, but I was in pain and unable to sleep.

I took in every story within the book. I had come to understand that timing played a crucial role. With the book held against my chest, I laid in bed and looked at Kingston's altar. I asked Kingston out loud again for a turtle, one I could physically hold rather than just see on my phone. I told him how much it would mean to me. I need you, yes you the reader, to take a moment and pause here with me.

I had hoped and prayed that the next day I would encounter a turtle in the streets or through a billboard advertisement—anything not confined to a digital screen. With no glimpse of hope or inkling of what was to come, I paused in this moment of plea, completely not prepared for the remarkable turn of events that awaited me.

I turned the page of my book at 12:29am.

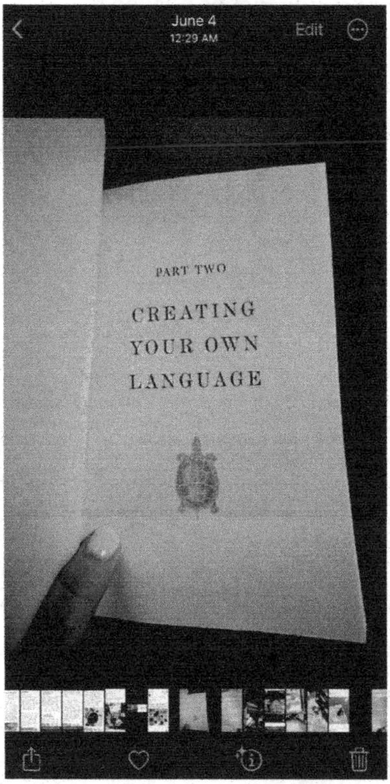

Let me be clear here. A turtle is not on the cover of this book. It has not been mentioned in any stories, and yet here it was in all its glory. In my hand with all capital letters with a title stating to me this is **our new language of love**. I burst into tears. I hugged the book close to my heart just sobbing. I took a picture to keep documenting my signs I received that day, and I went to sleep…right away.

The following morning, exhaustion clung to me as I stirred awake at 6am. Despite how tired I was, my eagerness to read compelled me. To my complete astonishment, as I turned the pages, I encountered yet another extraordinary moment. Kingston and Frank's names appeared on the same page, intertwined in a way that felt almost impossible. It became abundantly clear to me that I needed to reach out to Jinny. Thoughts raced through my mind as I contemplated how

I would tell Chris, knowing that he needed to hear and understand the profound experiences I had.

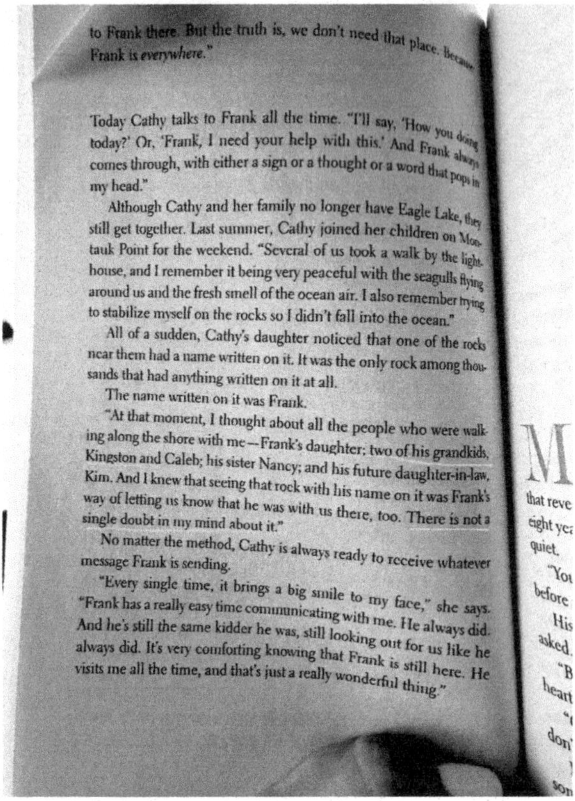

to Frank there. But the truth is, we don't need that place. Becau
Frank is *everywhere*."

Today Cathy talks to Frank all the time. "I'll say, 'How you doing today?' Or, 'Frank, I need your help with this.' And Frank always comes through, with either a sign or a thought or a word that pops in my head."

Although Cathy and her family no longer have Eagle Lake, they still get together. Last summer, Cathy joined her children on Montauk Point for the weekend. "Several of us took a walk by the lighthouse, and I remember it being very peaceful with the seagulls flying around us and the fresh smell of the ocean air. I also remember trying to stabilize myself on the rocks so I didn't fall into the ocean."

All of a sudden, Cathy's daughter noticed that one of the rocks near them had a name written on it. It was the only rock among thousands that had anything written on it at all.

The name written on it was Frank.

"At that moment, I thought about all the people who were walking along the shore with me—Frank's daughter; two of his grandkids, Kingston and Caleb; his sister Nancy; and his future daughter-in-law, Kim. And I knew that seeing that rock with his name on it was Frank's way of letting us know that he was with us there, too. There is not a single doubt in my mind about it."

No matter the method, Cathy is always ready to receive whatever message Frank is sending.

"Every single time, it brings a big smile to my face," she says. "Frank has a really easy time communicating with me. He always did. And he's still the same kidder he was, still looking out for us like he always did. It's very comforting knowing that Frank is still here. He visits me all the time, and that's just a really wonderful thing."

Chris started stirring and waking up. The kids were yawning and stretching, signaling the start of a new day. We got out of bed and made our way to brush our teeth. I stood at the sink looking in the mirror, thinking about how I would bring this up with Chris. I peeked over at him every now and then brushing his teeth. After rinsing my mouth and wiping it with a towel, I took a breath. I finally broke the silence and said, "Kingston has been talking to me. I need to talk to you about it." A pause. Then Chris said, "I have stuff to tell you as well." I squealed and said, "Tell me everything!" Chris told me to go get coffee and he would meet me in the hearth room, which is off our kitchen.

Sitting there in anticipation, I felt my heart ready to burst with excitement and a smile that wouldn't leave my face. I just knew Kingston had given him a turtle. With bated breath, I eagerly listened as Chris began to share what had transpired the night before while he was upstairs playing Call of Duty. He explained that the game had recently released a new character, prompting him to check it out and make adjustments to his avatar. Upon finishing updating his avatar and seeing the face of the new character, it made him laugh. He immediately thought of a funny meme. He started chuckling and began to say, "I like..." but before he could even complete the sentence, he burst into laughter and then a few tears, rolling his eyes in amusement, realizing that this was exactly how our little boy would find a way to reach him. And with that realization, he finally exclaimed, "...turtles!" It turned out that the meme he was referring to centered around turtles. For those unfamiliar with it, a quick Google search would provide the details.

Chris said after we had talked, and as he thought about what the medium said. He realized the importance of opening his mind to signs, and he couldn't believe he had verbalized his thoughts out loud. He also said that very night, Kingston visited him in his dream. There is a belief that if you're able to recognize in the dream that your loved one is no longer with you, it signifies a true visitation rather than a memory. In Chris's dream, he saw Kingston on the bed, initially unable to see him, but as he reached out and touched him, Kingston became visible. They shared a joyous and heartfelt moment, just as they used to do during our family nights in bed. When Chris woke up, tears streamed down his face, as he knew in his heart that his son had come to see him.

We just sat there taking it all in, awaiting our friend Mallory who was coming over. She had been to a store close by that morning and decided to stop by and check on us. We shared everything that had unfolded with her, recounting the incredible series of events. Mallory paused, and then she revealed something that left us all in awe—she had seen a turtle near our house that very morning. In *Signs*, I read that these messages do not just come directly to you, but at times they come through those around you. It was a powerful moment, serving as the final confirmation that I had been on the right path, even before Chris and Mallory knew, as I had already sent the text to Jinny earlier that morning. Filled with a sense of peace in my heart, I glanced out the window, smiling at the sky, knowing that Kingston was watching over us. Lost in my thoughts, I let my gaze wander, and as I brought my attention back into the room, I lowered my eyes and there it was—the toy turtle, another tangible manifestation of the signs and love that surrounded us.

Jinny replied to my text that morning about the medium. Her reply was beautiful. She had been crying ever since receiving my message and took time to collect herself before texting back. She shared that she had no doubt in her heart that their "little bubs, Frank" is with Kingston. She shared it would be three years on June 8th since they held him in their arms for the last time. She also shared she hadn't received any signs from him or visits in her dreams for a while. She thanked me for sharing with her because she believed it was his way of letting her know he is still with her. It was a beautiful exchange and it reinforced what I read in *SIGNS* that sometimes WE ourselves are the sign to pass along the love and light.

10

Edmond's Battle: Surviving and Balancing Work

If you remember from earlier, Edmond was scheduled to undergo an X-ray for a leg issue. The appointment had been set weeks in advance and happened to fall on the day after Kingston's passing. Chris and I were in such a state of grief and brokenness that we simply couldn't bear the thought of taking Edmond in for the X-ray. Given that it wasn't an urgent matter, we made the decision to call the vet that morning and reschedule the appointment. When we reached out, our veterinarian understood our emotional state, having been at our house the day before and witnessed what had occurred. They kindly rescheduled the X-ray for the following week.

Six days passed, and we were scheduled to take Edmond in for his X-ray the next day. I felt a sense of anxiety overwhelming me. I always worry about surgery and general anesthesia. While this X-ray wouldn't involve surgery, it still required the use of general anesthesia. I wasn't ready to entrust our son to the care of others and leave him there for the X-rays. The night before, following the guidance from the book *SIGNS*, I had asked Kingston out loud for a sign, a reassurance that he would watch over Edmond during the procedure. If you did not read the last section, the turtle became a sign for us with Kingston. That night I received a video of a turtle within my social media feed, but the hint of doubt still lingered. I wondered if it was merely an algorithmic coincidence since I had previously "liked" other turtle-related content.

Then something unexpected happened. In a photography group I had joined years ago, when I started PETraits by Erika, a post caught my attention. It was a serious post from someone seeking feedback on how to make an image look more realistic. In this group, everyone possessed professional-grade skills. Despite my own expertise in being able to swap heads and photoshopping leashes out of images, I had only posted in that group once before. So, it was quite surprising to see an image posted there that appeared unreal. But there it was—a turtle positioned protectively over a baby, symbolizing my son. The love I felt for Kingston overwhelmed me in that moment. Oh, my dear Kingston, how much I cherished and missed him. Here he was still being our protector.

Amy Lynn · 3h
Just playing around in photoshop, but something seems off. Skin tone or depth or contrast, I've been looking at it too long I think lol. Any tips? Thank you!
7
33 comments
Like
Comment
Send

I really felt for the person who had posted the image, as the comments left by others were far from kind. Some saying "I don't mean to be rude, but I don't understand the concept here. Why would a turtle crush a baby into the sand?" and "No offense intended, but what's off to me is the concept" and "is the turtle eating the kid". But for me it was clear. Intrigued, I clicked into the account and noticed that this individual had never posted before. Their profile gave off an artificial vibe, almost as if it were generated by a bot. What made it even more fascinating was the name associated with the account—Amy Lynn. It struck me as significant because Amy Lynn is one of the Shar Pei moms who had played a role in helping me come up with the name for this very book. The synchronicity of it all left me astounded and wondering about the deeper connections at play.

Kingston was truly communicating with us directly. I needed this. Although the X-ray was not considered urgent or an emergency, I was still contemplating whether we should proceed with it or cancel altogether. However, there was a significant reason why we ultimately decided to go ahead. Back in April, Edmond had experienced four episodes of fever within an eight-day span. Concerned, we submitted fecal and urine samples, which all came back normal. We also scheduled an appointment, during which a comprehensive blood panel was conducted. This type of bloodwork is more extensive, as it is sent off to a lab and takes longer to process. The results came back normal, but during the examination, our veterinarian discovered that Edmond's left leg was popping in and out of socket. There were suspicions of serious arthritis in his right leg, as evident from the cracking sounds during movement. To confirm the diagnosis, an X-ray was necessary.

For those who may not be familiar, when it comes to animals, the use of general anesthesia is required for X-rays. It is important for me to note that general anesthesia is not a routine or ordinary procedure. In my line of work, I frequently interact with healthcare providers, and I vividly recalled an anesthesiologist once telling me, "My job is to bring someone right to the brink of death and then keep them stable and alive." Additionally, while reading the *SIGNS* book, I came across a heartbreaking story about a boy who tragically lost his life during a dental procedure while under general anesthesia. These experiences and insights weighed heavily on my mind as I thought about Edmond's upcoming procedure.

We needed to get this X-ray though, as it was suspected he may need surgery and he was currently on a pain pill every day. We wanted to cancel it so badly. Edmond seemed "okay" and with the pain medicine seemed like he was doing fine. I thought maybe I could talk to the doctor about just keeping him on a daily pain regimen. I remembered those Bayer back and body commercials stating to take one every day. Couldn't Edmond just do the same? Chris and I talked that night and we both agreed we needed to take him in, and that Kingston would watch over him. Plus, Kingston had just given me a CLEAR sign.

I posted on Instagram to ask for the power of prayer around the world. I mentioned reading the book *SIGNS* and how Chris had chosen a turtle as our sign. It was important to me that our followers knew Kingston was communicating to us with turtles, and we truly believed that they were real. I explained that we had specifically asked Kingston to send me a sign that he would be present with Edmond on that day. I shared my anxiousness around anesthesia, explaining that the idea of putting any of our pups under anesthesia filled me with anxiety. I let our followers know that one day, I would share in more detail the remarkable signs we had been receiving from Kingston. (It feels amazing to finally be able to share our experiences—hello, Instagram and Facebook family!)

We thanked our followers, again, for being with us. Acknowledged having a Shar Pei is not easy. They require a community to lean on; a network of fellow Shar Pei parents that we could ask questions of and compare experiences, and a heart to lean on when you see how awful it is for them when they fever. Some fevers can spike to 104.4 and you can tell it's painful for them. With four pups, and now only three, it feels like we're always having something happening. However, despite the challenges, we wholeheartedly love our Shar Peis and feel honored to be their parents. Lastly, we made a promise to keep everyone updated on the results of Edmond's X-ray.

After we dropped off Edmond, nervousness consumed me throughout the day. As noon arrived, I still hadn't received a call. By 2pm, my anxiety levels were soaring. I texted Chris, asking if they had called yet. He responded, informing me that they hadn't started the procedure until 2pm, alleviating some of my worries.

At 2:46pm I received a text from Chris that said, "Just heard about Edmond. He is doing fine, but call me when you get off your call."

What the hell kind of text message was that? I couldn't get downstairs fast enough, so I called him. Chris answered and explained that they had discovered a dime-sized mass on the back of Edmond's tongue and removed it. He went on and said although it didn't appear aggressive, a biopsy would be necessary to determine if benign or malignant. I asked Chris to come up to my office. As soon as he walked in, tears streamed down my face. How could this be happening? Edmond had gone in for an X-ray to investigate suspected arthritis and the clicking sounds in his back legs that were identified a couple of months ago. There was no sense of urgency for the X-rays from the vet. I had been anxious about the anesthesia, but I held onto the belief that Kingston was watching over Edmond. Never did I imagine that cancer would be a possibility! It was not on my radar at all!

Chris sat with me as we anxiously anticipated the call to pick up Edmond. When our veterinarian finally called, he explained the situation once again. Edmond had done well during the procedure. While he did have arthritis in both legs, it could be managed with medication. However, they discovered a dime-sized tumor that was only visible because Edmond was under anesthesia, and they were cleaning his back teeth. The veterinarian couldn't say for certain if it was cancer or not, but they felt optimistic about what had been removed. By Monday, we would know if the tumor was benign or malignant. If it was benign, it wouldn't be a big concern. I asked about the possibility of cancer, wondering if it would be similar to Kingston's case. The veterinarian explained that if it was cancer, it would likely be an aggressive form due to its size and location. However, he reassured me that it was too early to be overly concerned and that further assessment would be needed.

We headed to go pick up our blue boy. Of course, I'm googling mouth and tongue cancers in canines the entire drive there. As we arrived, we were asked to come back behind the front desk to a room we've never been in before. We didn't even know exam rooms were in the back. For eight years we've been coming to this office and always thought there were only the five exam rooms up front, of which we have been in every single one. We walked in and waited. As we waited, I saw a picture of a manatee on the wall. We always joke that Edmond looks like one. Chris just stood still waiting, I kept searching the room and that's when I saw the door. A TURTLE.

In that moment, I felt Kingston's love and light around us. I showed it to Chris, and he gasped too. And boy did we need it. Before Edmond was brought in, they showed us photos of the tumor and even brought in the actual tumor itself. As a helicopter parent who works in healthcare, I have a tendency to ask a lot of questions and request detailed reports for any medical procedures or tests.

However, I must admit that my understanding of measurements seemed to falter at that moment. I'm either not good at understanding measurements or have a completely warped sense of what the hell "dime size" meant. This was massive.

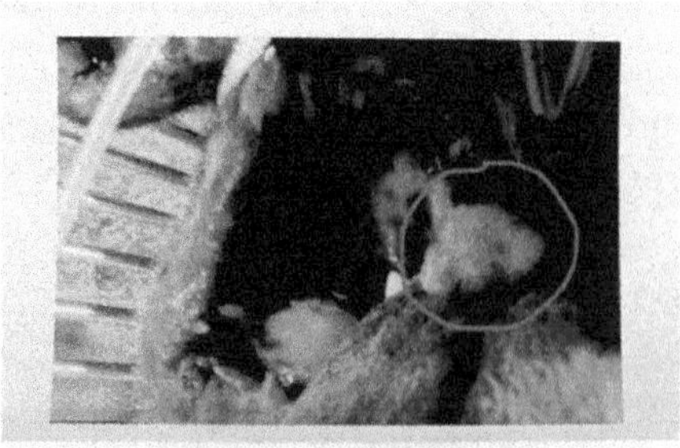

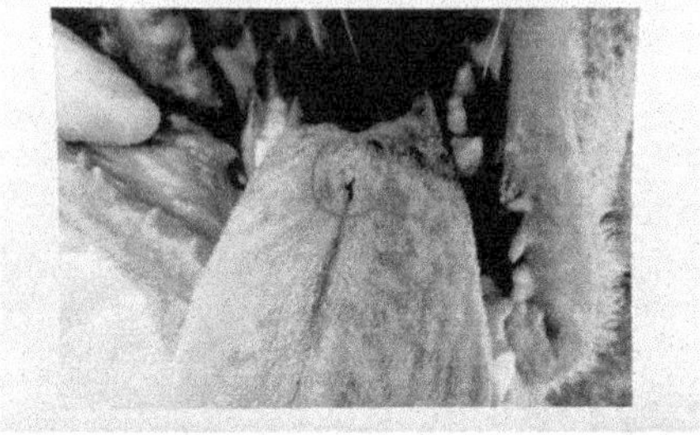

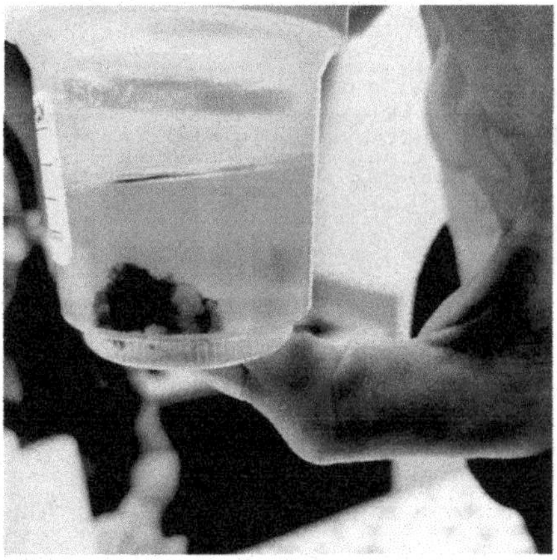

How could something of this size have been inside Edmond? How long had it been there? Had he been in pain all this time? My tension and worry were evident, and the nurse reassured me that the tumor hadn't been present during Edmond's teeth cleaning the previous year. It was possible that it had been growing steadily all that time. I immediately felt guilt.

The day after Kingston's passing, we had initially scheduled the X-ray, but we couldn't bring ourselves to take Edmond in for it. Then

I felt even more guilt as I thought back to the medium call where he also mentioned Edmond's leg which should have sparked the X-ray appointment. We were still consumed by raw pain and grief at that point and rescheduled his appointment. Did we make a mistake? Had we lost precious time, those fourteen days, during which this tumor could have been growing? I voiced my concerns to the nurse, who tried to offer some reassurance by suggesting that the tumor may not have been there initially and could have grown during that fourteen-day period. However, this did not make me feel better.

She left us to go get Edmond, and once again, my gaze was drawn to the turtle on the door. It was the only thing that calmed us so we could be in better energy for Edmond. We brought him home and then the waiting game began. We had to wait until Monday, six long days of not knowing stretched out before us.

I tried to go to work the next morning as if all was normal. I even had a session with my trainer that morning. I managed to make it through most of the workout, but towards the end, I felt overwhelmed. During the last two squats I said I couldn't, that I was going to vomit. I ran upstairs, leaving my him to let himself out. My body was trembling. I hovered the toilet. I couldn't breathe. I worked on my breathing to calm myself down. Edmond and Teddy came to check on me. I emailed my team to cancel my 8am meeting and stepped into the shower, determined to power through the day. However, after just two hours at my desk, the trembling returned, and I knew I couldn't continue. I finally called it. I told my leadership team I would be taking the rest of the day off and would not be reachable by phone. I felt like a raw exposed nerve flailing in the wind and every gust was painful. I crawled into bed, cuddled with Edmond, and let myself cry. My adrenaline and nervous system were completely shot. If I was a camel, this was the straw that broke my back.

In bed, I felt something. I sat up and grabbed my laptop and wrote these words to you for three hours. I needed to let it all out. It struck me deeply in my heart how important it is to acknowledge and normalize the very real pain of losing a pet and now the uncertainty of Edmond's future.

Over the past 21 days since Kingston's passing, I had been struggling with my emotions, attempting to navigate work and maintain a positive outlook. It felt as though no one at work truly understood the depths of my pain. Prior to returning from my company's pet bereavement leave, I reached out to my vice president on my leadership team in an attempt to figure out how to re-engage with my team. In a text, I expressed that I was not in a position to engage in small talk. That I couldn't bear the thought of being asked, "how was your weekend?" at the start of every single meeting for seven hours straight. I wanted grace and I wanted my employees to know that I may not show up as my bubbly self.

With completely pure intentions, this was instead communicated and perceived by employees to "pretend nothing happened" like…at all. Not just when interacting with me at work, but as a whole. This explained why in 21 days since Kingston's passing, I had received limited contact from my team.

I had, for the past 21 days, felt a sense of shame for how I was handling the situation. I questioned my own ability to manage grief and wondered if I was fulfilling my role as a CEO. As a woman CEO, I already wonder if I'm are doing a good job and would a man or someone else do it better. The weight of expectation pressed upon me, fueling self-doubt and aching vulnerability. I wondered if my handling of the pain, the loss, was somehow inadequate. The absence of flowers at all from my team, or even a simple message saying they were thinking of us left me shattered and validated in how I was feeling.

Shame and isolation took over my heart, as I questioned whether I had failed to foster the empathetic environment I so relentlessly believed in. Throughout my years of leadership, I had painstakingly woven a tapestry of care and support, cultivating a culture that embraced the intricacies of our lives beyond the confines of our job titles. Protocols were established, guiding our actions when moments of celebration or despair touched our lives. Flowers to commemorate milestones, promotions, a new baby, pregnancy news, bark boxes to welcome furry family members, and heartfelt donations to honor beloved pets who passed—each gesture tenderly crafted, affirming the essence of our shared humanity. Yet, amidst the raw anguish I was weathering, it seemed these threads of compassion had unraveled.

To give you some insight of these protocols and how they are placed I'll share with you a moment when I learned that one of our employees had an issue with a paycheck during their maternity leave. I was told there was "there was a paperwork problem that had worked itself out" message. Once understanding the full situation, I was furious. Furious not only that it happened, how it was communicated to me, but also the resolution being proposed to avoid this happening in the future was not enough. I immediately set up a meeting with Human Resources and Operations to address the issue.

In that meeting, I was met with some resistance. There was a notion that it wasn't the company's responsibility to ensure employees complete the paperwork, as we would still pay the remaining percentage to make the employee whole. I couldn't stay silent, and although my blood was boiling inside, I calmly explained that these are significant life events happening for our employees. A new human life has entered the world, and we needed to take it seriously. We should be proactive in sending the necessary forms, obtaining a point of contact that we text while they are still in the hospital given the form has to be signed there, and even consider making it a fun moment by sending a onesie along with sending physical copies of the form for the hospital "go bag". I emphasized that we should go above and beyond to support our employees during these important moments.

Ironically, this meeting was just a week prior to the passing of my beloved Kingston. As the CEO who established these types of rules and values, I couldn't help but feel a deep disappointment when I didn't receive even a bouquet of flowers from my own company honoring Kingston and what we were going through.

However, on that Tuesday, when I found out about Edmond's situation and was told that I had to wait until the following Monday for a possible cancer diagnosis, my body couldn't handle it anymore. I reached my breaking point and decided to prioritize my well-being. After abruptly ending my day, one of the consultants who had sent me flowers after Kingston passed, text me to call her as a friend. That call became a turning point as I poured out all my emotions and frustrations. She understood every bit of it.

Little did I know that the consultant would then reach out to my vice presidents. Within an hour, I received a text from my leadership team informing me that they had cleared the rest of my week. They acknowledged the weight of the situation and said that they knew it would be difficult for me. They understood that it was a lot to bear. I was speechless. Through tears, I replied expressing my gratitude for their proactive support. It meant so much to me that I didn't have to prove myself or justify my struggles. My leadership team was genuinely looking out for me. I shared that I had been carrying a sense of shame for how poorly I felt I was handling everything. With Kingston's passing and now Edmond's health concerns, I felt like an exposed raw nerve, vulnerable and sensitive to the world around me.

This is the reply I received from my leadership team:

> *Expel the shame from your heart. That's not an emotion you should be feeling right now. I was calling earlier to let you know how often, and broadly, and how sincerely nearly everyone asks about you and Chris. Ryan asks me daily if I have an update on how you are. We decided early on to try to shield you from it in an effort to not expose you to constant reminders of the sadness and then be burdened with consoling others about their own feelings of remorse. We also decided that I would share updates with the team so that you weren't having to repeat yourself and relieve it constantly (as I'm sure the rest of the world is bombarding you with questions).*

> *I'm really sorry if that translated into a situation where you felt isolated, unloved, unseen or anything that doesn't equate to love, care and concern that is truly overflowing just out of sight. No one wants you to relive what is probably one of your worst days. But everyone is here for you should you need to. And if you need more time than just Thur/Friday that is completely okay. Ryan and I got this. It won't be the same without you and we do need you, but we can absolutely do this for as long as necessary without you. You and Chris should have the time and space you need. I will handle the meetings above. Go do what you two need to do.*

Just tears. I poured my heart out in gratitude, expressing how their understanding and support meant the world to me. I couldn't find the words to thank them enough for allowing me the time and space to be with Edmond and to take care of myself during this difficult waiting period. The thought of facing the uncertainty until Monday, when we would receive the news about Edmond's condition, was overwhelming. Their gesture gave me the opportunity to be present for Edmond, Mishka and Teddy; to take long walks, to cry, and to rest. It was a lifeline in my time of need.

I assured them that I would keep them informed on Monday once we knew the results. If it turned out not to be cancer, I would return to work, but with a focus on lighter meeting schedules and a gentler approach towards myself. However, if the news was cancer, I explained that we would need to take things one day at a time. In my vulnerable state, I shared with them how broken I felt, and their willingness to accommodate my needs was truly touching. It was a reminder of the importance of empathy and understanding in the workplace, and I was deeply grateful for their compassion.

He replied, "*We will be ready to support you, no matter what happens. Even if, and hopefully it's good news, we are going to plan on you being out longer than Monday. It takes more than a day to recover from this fight or flight life you're leading.*"

That night we watched Ted Lasso finale with Mishka, Edmond and Teddy. Chris was trying out taking 10mg of Melatonin. He had not been able to sleep a full night the last 21 days. I sat in gratitude from the day and the love I felt from my team. We went to bed at 9pm. Chris went right to sleep. I could not. My mind just started racing. I missed Kingston, I was thinking about Edmond, and I was reconciling my feelings and revelations about the support structures we need at work.

Time seemed to stretch on, but I refused to pick up my phone or read. I needed to sleep. It wasn't until my phone chimed with a notification that I realized how much time had passed. I typically keep my phone on silent during the night, but for some reason, the sound was on. Curiosity got the better of me, and I picked up my phone to see a text message from my dear friend Audrey. It was unusual for her to message me at this hour, knowing that I typically go to bed early. The text contained a photo, and I eagerly opened it to see what she had sent.

It truly felt like a magical moment orchestrated by Kingston himself, how he managed to deliver a turtle to me even when I had refused to pick up my phone. And the fact that Audrey happened to be awake at that hour, on a different time zone, enjoying dessert with a turtle on it—it was a synchronicity that filled me with awe. How could anyone deny the existence of magic after experiencing something like this?

I want to take a moment to acknowledge my privilege as a CEO and business owner, and the support I received from my team to take time off and provide the necessary care for myself and my family. I am grateful for these opportunities, knowing that not everyone has access to such support in their workplaces. While I understand that it may not be possible to replicate this level of assistance across all industries and roles, I know that there is always something that can be done to show compassion and understanding.

This realization has been the driving force behind the workplace resource section that you'll find at the end of this book. I am inspired to advocate for pets to be included in bereavement policies. By shedding light on this often-overlooked aspect of grief, we can create a more empathetic society and drive positive change within organizations. I want to ignite a conversation and bring awareness to the profound bond between humans and their beloved pets. I want organizations to consider incorporating pet bereavement leave in their policies.

I also was inspired to provide training and resources to help employees navigate pet bereavement leave and to support their return to work. Perhaps it starts with simple gestures, like refraining from asking generic questions such as "how are you?" or "how was your weekend?", and instead offering genuine acknowledgement and grace. I compiled a comprehensive training guide, complete with scripts and sample texts, to aid individuals in their own personal journeys or to provide support to those they care about.

Losing a pet can be a deeply emotional experience, and the grief that follows is real and significant. It's essential for employers to recognize the bond between humans and their pets and acknowledge the impact that their loss can have on an individual's well-being.

In Part 5 workplace section at the end of this book, I have included a resource specifically designed to help you advocate for pet bereavement leave in your own workplace. This resource provides compelling statistics that highlight the impact of pet loss on employees and the workplace. It also offers practical guidance on how to approach the conversation with Human Resources, including an FAQ document to help navigate common concerns and objections.

Together, we can raise awareness and make change about the importance of pet bereavement support in the workplace and work towards creating a more compassionate and understanding environment for those who have experienced the loss of a beloved pet. Let's strive for change and ensure that employees receive the support and understanding they need during this challenging time.

(My incredible team)

11

The Relentless Fight: Confronting Cancer Once Again

After six days of watching Kingston hurt, have his heart drained, and then losing him, the worst pain of my life began. Then, 21 days later, June 6th I went from feeling Kingston was watching over Edmond to being completely caught off guard. During those six days of waiting to hear if Edmond had cancer, my emotions were on a rollercoaster. The pain of losing Kingston was still fresh in my heart, and now the news of Edmond's tumor added another layer of fear and uncertainty. It was a delicate balance between grieving for Kingston and worrying about Edmond's health.

To distract ourselves, we made a conscious effort to create moments of joy. We took the kids on walks in the mornings, cherishing the simple act of being together and soaking in the beauty of nature. The summer heat couldn't deter us; we knew we had to be there for our kids who were also feeling the loss of Kingston. During one of these walks at our favorite park, we were surprised to spot a real turtle in the water. As we strolled along the path, we noticed all the little educational signs, provided by the St. Louis Library, had turtles on them—every single one. This synchronicity was remarkable, and the signs we learned are changed each month. It felt like more than mere chance—it was a comforting reminder that Kingston's presence was still surrounding us, guiding us through our difficult journey.

While our minds were consumed with worry, those few moments gave my heart a break from the overwhelming pain of missing Kingston. I held onto the signs of turtles that Kingston had sent, seeking comfort and reassurance that he was still watching over us. Each day felt like an eternity as we waited for the biopsy results, and the weight of the unknown loomed over us. But we held onto hope, relying on the love and support of our family and friends to carry us through this challenging time.

My phone rang that Monday. Chris and I were in the kitchen. I sat down and put the phone on the table and on speaker. My heart sank as our veterinarian confirmed the devastating news. Edmond had malignant melanoma, an aggressive form of cancer. The shock and disbelief overwhelmed me, and I could hear the pain in our veterinarian's voice as he delivered the diagnosis. I thanked him for calling, but the weight of those words felt crushing.

Chris slowly crumbled to the floor, and I found myself in a daze. The familiar waves of grief washed over me, and I couldn't help but collapse onto the carpet, the screams escaping my throat. It was a raw, gut-wrenching pain that consumed me once again.

As I regained some semblance of awareness, anger surged through me. The tears stopped, and a surge of energy propelled me to my feet. I knew I needed to take immediate action. I texted my team, explaining that I wasn't sure when I would return, as our focus now shifted to finding an oncologist for Edmond. Chris retreated to our bedroom, seeking comfort in our bed. Meanwhile, I frantically began calling local oncologists, desperate for an appointment. But the earliest availability I could find was in August. I just knew we couldn't wait that long.

I reached out to our veterinarian in tears, and he suggested contacting Mizzou University. I called and they offered a consult appointment on July 18th. It was over a month away, but it was the best we could find. I scheduled the appointment as a safety net, but determined, I continued my search, reaching out to the top veterinary oncology institutions across the country.

In the midst of my frantic efforts, I had a thought to share our journey on Instagram. The outpouring of support and love from our community was astounding. I shared the devastating news, our shattered state, and the urgent need for an oncologist. I poured my heart out, expressing our desperation and the lengths we were willing to go for Edmond's care.

And then, a glimmer of hope emerged. A follower named Heather reached out, connecting us with an oncologist recommended by her friend on the state board of veterinary medicine in South Carolina. It felt like a lifeline. This oncologist could see us the following week.

The power of community and the kindness of strangers became our guiding force. In that moment, I felt a renewed sense of hope and determination. We were not alone in this fight, and with their support, we would do everything in our power to give Edmond the best care possible.

I called, made the appointment, and started making travel plans. However, thirty minutes later, they called back, seemingly astonished by the distance we would have to travel and wanted to ensure I knew they were in South Carolina. I quickly said, "yes" to which they responded, "yes, but do you know how far that is?" At the same time, we said "ten hours and thirty-four minutes". Through tears, I reassured them that I understood and explained the urgency of the situation, sharing the heartbreaking loss of Kingston. They expressed their condolences and assured me that they looked forward to meeting us the following week.

Overwhelmed with emotions I sat at our kitchen table with tears of joy then I headed to wake Chris up and share the news. But before I even reached the living room, my phone rang once more. It was the South Carolina office again. They informed me that they had spoken to the oncologist about our situation and the distance we would be traveling. Remarkably, he was willing to do a phone consultation if we could provide the pathology report, tumor images, and chest X-rays to assess the extent of the cancer's spread. I could hardly believe it. I assured them that I would get all the necessary things as quickly as possible and get back to them.

With tears streaming down my face, I called our veterinarian to share the news. I asked when we could come in to obtain the required tests. To my surprise, the front desk came back on the line and said, "Can you come today at 6? He said he would stay late to make this happen." My heart swelled with gratitude for the incredible support we were receiving. I called the South Carolina office again to let them know that we would have everything sent over that night. In response, they informed me that the oncologist would conduct our consultation the next day at 2pm ET via Zoom.

I felt real hope. Within hours of receiving the devastating cancer diagnosis, we were being seen by professionals who were willing to go above and beyond for us. It was an extraordinary turn of events made possible by the power of community, love, and compassion.

That next day Chris and I gathered in our kitchen for the Zoom call, with Edmond by our side. The oncologist joined the call and asked if we could see him. His camera was dark then it lit up and he said he could finally see us. He admitted that he had never done a virtual consultation before, but he was glad he could offer his assistance. He then requested to see Edmond. We brought the laptop down to the floor and sat beside Edmond. The oncologist reviewed the X-rays, expressing that they looked good and there were no signs of cancer spreading to the lungs. He proceeded to share his thoughts on the pathology report and provided his recommendations.

He conveyed a sense of optimism, explaining that we had caught the cancer early. If we could begin treatment within the next two weeks, he believed we had a real chance at fighting it. We expressed our gratitude for his expertise and for taking the time to help us. In that moment, we clung to the hope and possibility that lay before us, united in our determination to do everything in our power to save Edmond's life.

The next four hours were a flurry of phone calls as I followed up with the institutions I had reached out to the day before. There were better options than our only scheduled appointment at MIZZOU like at Wisconsin University who could fit us in on July 11th, but that was a month away and we needed within 2 weeks. I decided to give the University of Illinois another try, and this time, the scheduler for another department offered to personally speak with the oncology scheduler on my behalf. I waited anxiously for an hour before calling back. She assured me again that the oncology scheduler would call me back. I couldn't help but break down in tears, apologizing for my urgency and explaining the overwhelming situation. She couldn't believe what we were going through and promised again that she would call me back either that day or the next. Unfortunately, I didn't receive a call that day.

The next day was my first therapy session, and I was grateful to have it on the calendar as I continued to wait for an appointment. I informed my therapist that I was waiting for an important call that it might come during our session. Halfway through the session, my phone rang, and I answered, putting it on speaker and trembling with anticipation. It was the University of Illinois. The oncology scheduler was on the line, and she began by saying that she owned a Shar Pei too and understood our urgency. She mentioned that they could try to fit us in, and then she said, "June..." I burst into tears of relief before she could even tell me the date. I just heard June. She comforted me, assuring me that they would find a way to accommodate us. She suggested June 26th, and I couldn't contain my overwhelming joy and gratitude. Through tears, I expressed my heartfelt gratitude, and she said she couldn't wait to meet us. She promised to email me a confirmation of everything. Not only had we secured an appointment at a top institution, but it was also the closest one, just a 3.5-hour drive away, and it was within the two-week window.

Filled with hope and relief, I finished my therapy session and drove home feeling like I was floating on a cloud. I sang "The Climb" by Miley Cyrus at the top of my lungs, embracing the newfound positivity. But as I drove home, my phone rang again. I answered, surprised to hear an oncologist from the University of Illinois on the other end. He mentioned that he understood we needed to come in for our dog, who had confirmed tongue cancer. I confirmed this and informed him that I had just spoken to the scheduler and had an appointment for the 26th. He seemed unaware of this and mentioned that he was returning my call from a voicemail I had left on Monday.

He began discussing trials. I asked if we could pursue radiation, as recommended by the South Carolina oncologist, alongside a trial. He informed me that trials would exclude radiation, but possibly we could still pursue the immunotherapy. I expressed my hesitation towards experimental treatments, acknowledging I understood the importance of clinical trials given my own career in healthcare and I knew this is how innovation and new important therapies are born, but asserting my firm stance on proceeding with radiation. He calmly understood my position and mentioned that if I was willing to discuss the trial, they could potentially get us in earlier. I couldn't help but feel frustrated and asked, "So you're willing to see me earlier if I talk about a trial, but you can't get me in without discussing it?" He started to explain the trial again and its potential impact, and that's when I broke down. With tears and gripping the steering wheel tightly, I exclaimed, "I'm NOT DOING A TRIAL. If you're okay with me coming, knowing I won't do it, let's schedule it so I can get my son in. I just lost my other son three weeks ago to heart cancer, and I'm not okay. I'm currently driving home from my therapy appointment, crying, while on a short-term prescription plan that honestly I shouldn't even be able to generate tears right now." I could sense that I had startled him. He calmly replied, "Ma'am, I completely understand. Thank you again for taking my call." We ended the conversation, both of us hanging up.

I want to take a moment here to acknowledge that you, as a reader, may be thinking that you may not have had the tools or experience to navigate a conversation with a veterinary oncologist, or to realize that one office's appointment date isn't the only option available. If I hadn't worked in healthcare, I might not have known how to advocate for ourselves. I believe that my journey, both in my career and in experiencing this, has led me to a place where I can share these insights with the world. I want you to understand that simply by reading this book, you are already showing how much you love and care about your own pets or are a caring individual who wants to support others through tough times. My instincts I truly believe were based on my professional background and guided our decisions. I also feel so lucky for our online community, which played a crucial role in Edmond's care. The support I received through the online community is what helped me recognize that our experiences can't be faced alone. This realization is at the core of why this book is so important to me. We need community, and that's a message that needs to reach more pet parents, so they can reach out to their family and friends and feel supported during these challenging moments versus feeling shame.

Getting home I was filled with a mixture of emotions. The calmness came when I checked my email. At the top of my inbox was the email confirmation of our June 26th appointment. I replied with gratitude and included our family photo. I wanted them to see the family they were giving hope to. In that moment, I just wanted us to not be another patient, but to humanize us and truly thank them for their care and urgency.

The following day, I received a call from the University of Illinois, and the woman on the line seemed excited to speak with me. She mentioned that an oncologist from the clinical trials department had specifically called her to see if they could get us in sooner. She also said, "Also, thank you so much for sending that beautiful photo of your family to our scheduler. We are all looking at it. It's so beautiful. What a pack you have!"

I told her that we lost the gold one 3 weeks ago due to heart cancer, which only gave us six days notice. She said, "Oh my honey. That is too much to handle too fast. Did you tell the doctor that? This must be why. Oh, honey we all can't wait to meet you all and Edmond next week. We know it's a drive so let's try to schedule, consult, and do the CT scan the SAME day. We can't do radiation that day, but we could the following week, so it ALL will be starting a FULL week earlier."

That day became a turning point for me. I felt a sense of relief knowing that I had done everything within my power to secure the best possible care for Edmond and sheer gratitude to have so much love and support around me. I truly could not fathom how any pet parent could have gone through this alone.

That day I had also previously scheduled a tattoo appointment. It was the first day in three weeks that I put on makeup and ventured out for something unrelated to veterinary appointments and waiting anxiously for results. I felt a renewed sense of hope, knowing that we were taking every step necessary to give Edmond a real fighting chance.

After many discussions with Chris and finding the most beautiful place with a tattoo artist who specializes in "fine line tattoo", I went. There aren't many fine line tattoo artist, but here one was in St. Louis. WINK iboutique: lash & brow bar

Chris came with me. Everything about the experience was beautiful. I felt Kingston with me. This tattoo, to me, is a beautiful reminder of love. Every time it catches my eye, I smile and think of Kingston first and before the pang of pain hits I think of Edmond, Mishka and Teddy and keep smiling.

To have gotten a tattoo on that day and then receive the call that Edmond's therapy could be moved up by an entire week... it was undeniably one of the best days I had experienced in the last 30 days. Chris and I had made a pact to celebrate even the smallest victories and find joy in every moment. But on that particular day, the win was undeniably big, and it filled our hearts with hope and gratitude.

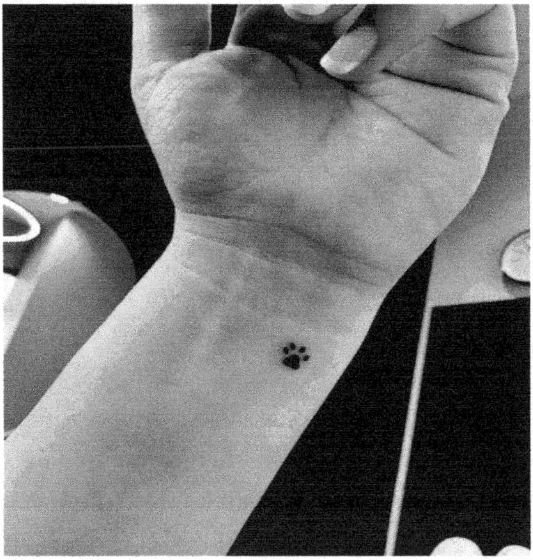

We were gearing up for the fight against Edmond's cancer. Having the appointment scheduled, I felt for the first time in a few weeks a sense of relief. It was in that moment that I just started sobbing. Only this time it felt like I could just cry without the guilt I was feeling about Kingston. Now having been fighting cancer again with Edmond, meeting with more oncologists, researching even more online, I could finally see how cancer is not just cancer. The types, where it's located, and especially the timing of when it is discovered is all relevant. I realized how lucky we were for Edmond's to be found so early in another procedure. With every passing day I was learning more and finally able to see that saving Kingston was just not possible. I could really start telling myself, and believe, that I could now grieve Kingston because I missed him, instead of how sorry I was I couldn't save him.

I shared the update about being able to get the appointment with my incredible leadership team, the very people who had been there with me since the inception of our company. They surprised me with an extraordinary gift - a "well-deserved sabbatical" they said. They insisted that heartache like this can qualify for short term leave and advocated that I take three months off, assuring me that they had everything under control. They anticipated my concerns and objections, presenting a comprehensive plan to address them. I felt an overwhelming sense of love and support from my team. It was a level of care that I had never experienced before. Though I just couldn't take the full three months, I agreed to a six-week break, grateful for the flexibility it would afford me during Edmond's treatment.

In addition to their extraordinary gesture, my team went above and beyond by sending us a card. Inside it, we found they had purchased 500 trees in Kingston's name, to be planted in Texas, where Kingston was born. The tears that welled up this time were not of sadness or joy, but rather a testament to the profound impact of their kindness. My heart was deeply moved.

We moved into week four of Edmond's journey. Our first appointment had been a significant milestone, as they were able to administer his first round of radiation and immunotherapy. Additionally, they performed a CT scan to confirm that the cancer had not spread to his chest and a cytology test to determine if it had affected his lymph nodes. The samples were sent off for pathology, and we anxiously awaited the results. Another four days of waiting. The call came in, and unfortunately, it was confirmed that the cancer had spread to one lymph node and likely the other, necessitating surgery to remove them.

We were told surgery is currently booked out through September, but our visits at the University of Illinois had left a lasting impression. They rallied behind us, saying we had "team Edmond" there. Through their efforts, they managed to schedule the surgery for July 6th.

On July 5th, we made the 3.5-hour drive, and met for the surgery consult. When we arrived for the surgery consult, Edmond underwent bloodwork and another CT scan to ensure that only the original top two lymph nodes were being removed, and that the cancer hadn't spread further. The veterinary team took extra time to explain the surgery in detail, even drawing a picture to help us understand. During his visit, Edmond had the opportunity to go for a walk with his assigned fourth-year student veterinarian who took a picture with him. It was an incredibly kind gesture, and we were touched when she texted the photo to us.

Throughout the process, they also managed to capture images of him during the CT scan.

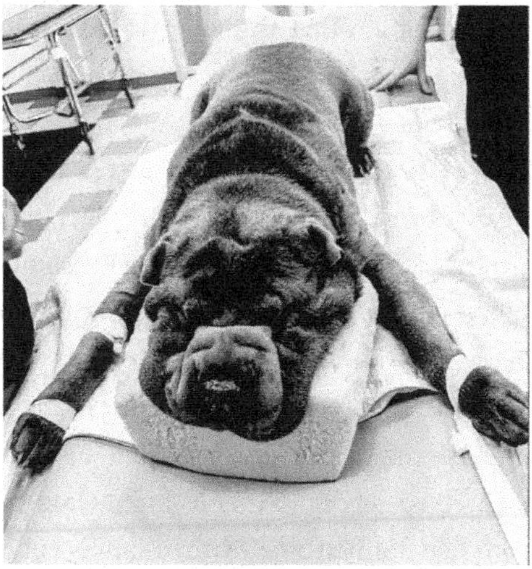

We felt so very connected to the University, the process, and the sense they also loved him. We wanted to express our immense gratitude to them. We went to Manolo's, the best pizza place in town we're told, and picked up several delicious pizzas to bring back to the university. When we presented the pizzas to the office team, their eyes lit up with surprise and gratitude. It was a small gesture compared to the incredible care they had provided to Edmond, but we wanted them to know just how thankful we were for their dedication, expertise, and care. In that moment, we realized that they, too, were grateful for us as this was not common. It was a beautiful exchange of gratitude and mutual appreciation.

Edmond was able to come back to the hotel with us that night. It was a difficult night. Edmond had been restless and did not sleep. We were up all night with him, trying to comfort him as he cried. He didn't like the hotel room, the light coming in from the city, or being away from Mishka and Teddy. He needed a potty break at midnight and again at 2am, which required getting in the car and driving to the park since the hotel did not have grass around it.

On Thursday, we dropped off Edmond at 7am, which was so hard. We knew that the surgery was necessary to save him, but leaving him until Friday hurt. I knew that Thursday would be a difficult day for me, so I had scheduled a virtual therapy session and another medium call to happen that day.

In preparation for the surgery, I also posted a few days prior on our social media platforms, asking everyone to wear blue on that day. I hoped that by seeing all the blue, it would bring me some comfort. And I have to say, it worked. We felt an overwhelming amount of love and support from everyone around us. We had pups and people dressed in blue all over the world. I shared every single one of them on our page.

Throughout the day, we anxiously awaited news about his progress. And then it arrived—a photo that brought tears to our eyes. The soft tissue students had donned blue attire in support of Edmond. They said they saw on our social media and knew to wear blue. It wasn't a complete gathering of all of them, but they managed to capture the moment with those who were available, including an IMC technician who cared deeply for Edmond. It was a gesture that meant the world to us. We felt incredibly fortunate to be surrounded by such compassionate human beings and to be able to see our son postoperatively.

The surgery took a bit longer than expected because they decided to remove all six lymph nodes. Once inside, they noticed that the two nodes they had initially planned to leave had unusual coloring. We were relieved to know that all the nodes were gone, and that the cancer had been successfully removed. The nodes were sent off for further analysis. We now had another six days of waiting ahead to learn the extent of the cancer's involvement.

Our next appointment is on July 21st, where we hope to receive a positive plan that involves only immunotherapy moving forward. The goal is for Edmond to receive immunotherapy at that appointment, followed by another session two weeks later, and then every six months for the rest of his life. It has been an exhausting and challenging journey, but we are determined to fight for Edmond's well-being. By the time this book is published, we hope that you will see our family still together and thriving on our social media platforms.

Until then, I want to again recognize just how incredible the entire team at University of Illinois really is. The extra care and attention they provided not only in treatment, but also at the front desk and in communications. During our time at the university, we couldn't help but overhear conversations from other pet parents who were struggling with the cost of care. Despite their deep love for their pets, they faced uncertainty about how they would be able to afford the necessary treatments. It was heartbreaking to witness their struggles, and we observed the front desk team doing their best to navigate these challenging situations. We couldn't imagine the emotional toll for all. We felt incredibly fortunate that we were able to provide for Edmond without financial hardship. The realization of this contrast filled our hearts with even more gratitude and compassion for those facing difficult decisions due to financial constraints.

During our time at the university, we also encountered families who received heartbreaking news and met other dogs who were not expected to survive much longer. Their pain resonated with us deeply, as we had experienced those emotions during Kingston's journey and still were unsure if our hearts would be breaking even more soon with Edmond. Witnessing their struggles reminded us to cherish every moment we had with Edmond and appreciate the incredible care provided by the doctors, nurses, front desk staff, and the entire veterinary team.

PART 4:

SHARING THE JOURNEY

12

Uniting in Grief: Connecting with Others Who Understand

Navigating the challenges of grief and dealing with cancer was a tough journey. My unique background in healthcare provided me with a toolkit that allowed me to navigate this difficult terrain more effectively. However, I want to emphasize that the actions I took were not mere instincts; they were shaped by my professional experience and the support of having an online community. It's important for anyone reading my story to understand that these actions are not inherent or instinctual – we all do the best we can in our own individual situations.

If you've read part 1, you're familiar with how I navigated life, often without the best judgment. It's so important to me that I emphasize a critical point - we're all human beings, trying our best. Throughout my book, a core theme is the significance of community support, coupled with the vital need for both giving and receiving kindness and compassion, especially to ourselves.

Advocating for ourselves often requires holding our ground, even when met with skepticism or dismissal. My background in healthcare, where my job is to help patients advocate for their needs, is what taught me these invaluable skills. Doctors can't possibly have all the answers for every individual circumstance. Over the years, I've developed patient discussion guides to help individuals prepare for their medical appointments. It's these experiences spanning two decades that offered me insights into managing my own situation with Kingston. My hope, through this book, is to pass on some of this wisdom by detailing how I applied these strategies in my own journey.

These strategies came in full force, when we rushed Kingston to the emergency room that first day and faced disbelief due to his normal eating and drinking. They actually said, "so wait he's eating and drinking? And yet you are here?" We stood our ground because we sensed something was amiss, and my profession has shown me the importance of listening to your body and recognizing when things aren't right. It's a lesson that emphasizes the value of seeking a second opinion and not accepting dismissals. This resolve extended to requests like asking to see Kingston's cancer diagnosis X-rays rather than simply being told about it. I pushed for a copy and a thorough explanation, an action that proved critical for me in comprehending the gravity of the situation. The reality hit harder when I could visually grasp the magnitude of what we were facing. Just six days before, Kingston had been seemingly healthy, a stark contrast to the harsh reality confronting us.

Recognizing the significance of not settling for the first available appointment for Edmond's treatment was a pivotal lesson. My professional background, centered around assisting patients in accessing necessary care and securing second opinions, underscored the importance of this choice. If not for this experience, we might have waited for the MIZZOU appointment, which we know now would have been too late. Not that MIZZOU didn't seem to share the same urgency for an earlier appointment, but their availability simply did not allow for it. Without my experience I truly would have believed this was the best we could do.

Lastly, my understanding of the urgency was solely prompted by the oncology visit, during which we were advised to initiate treatment within the next two weeks for a fighting chance. The role of our online community in facilitating this visit truly shows their instrumental support, a role for which we are eternally grateful and fully aware of how fortunate we are to have them. I am convinced that it was a higher purpose guiding my life's journey, leading me to write this book.

As I share my journey, I want everyone to know deeply that not taking these actions or having a different experience is perfectly okay. Each of us navigates challenging moments in the best way we can and know how. I am grateful for the life path that has led me to this point of sharing my experience with the world. Sharing my life's journey, from my early years to the profound grief that inspired this book, makes this meaningful. If it makes a difference in just one person's life, it's entirely worth it.

This realization is at the core of why this book is so important to me. We need to be kinder to ourselves, and we desperately need community. That's a message that needs to reach more pet parents, so they can feel supported during these challenging moments.

In the absence of readily available resources, it became evident that being proactive, asking questions, and advocating for our pets' well-being were essential in this journey. While the process was overwhelming at times, the validation that by sharing our journey helped others propelled us forward.

We received a Direct Message from one of our followers:

> *Our pup has been sick for a while and we're fairly private so we've hesitated telling anyone but close family and friends. My wife and I have been watching your journey. Your posts inspired us to tell everyone and, in a way, you've helped us prepare for what is to come (as much as that's possible). So, thank you. We're kind of at a loss of what to do with our other pup when the time comes.*
>
> *Should he be there? Should we leave him with a sitter? We have no idea as we've never gone through this before.*
>
> *Any words of advise you could give would be greatly appreciated*

I also was tagged in this post:

Caption: Happy 6th Birthday to my bru bru, my bubba, my big boy

In my arms, Bruno crossed the rainbow bridge on April 29th. It has been the longest month and a half of navigating the ebbs and flows of grief. Bruno was our first baby and the reason we fell in love with this breed. Picking him up in Canada and exploring Banff with him was the best adventure. Our life felt complete. There wasn't another lonely day. Everything soon became about him or for him.

Even though he was sick a lot, I hope the good memories outweighed the countless vet appointments. There are so many things I will miss:

- *tantrums he throws when he needs to go out*
- *nonstop pawing for chin/boop scratches until your fingers fall off*
- *how he taught both Benji and Penny how to pei-trol*
- *playing hide n seek & doing zoomies (5 min tops)*
- *his love for car rides, yogurt, bananas, bully sticks, and BREAD!*
- *how he stands by his bowl and side eyes you for new (filtered) water*
- *how he loves attention from strangers bc he knows he is handsome*
- *his growls at the door but in reality, would not hurt a fly*
- *his unforgettable love for Miss Shark from Ikea*
- *his dislikes for baths, ear cleanings, and the UPS truck that failed to deliver a Chewy package*
- *how he smells like Fritos*
- *the poo explosions in the house and the efforts to cover it up with Miss Shark*

The list goes on and I miss it all. Thank you baby boy for the best years of my life. I know you are having a kick ass time with your brother and all of your furry friends that are being deeply missed by their families. Thank you to my friends and family who have been there.

To everyone who has loved Bruno on IG. To @crazypei (our account on Instagram) who lost their beloved Kingston recently and has allowed me to go through this grieving journey with them. Lastly to Dr. Title, who is the most selfless person and a gift to this breed!

I asked them if I could share their story. They replied with,

> *"Of course you can include it All your posts for Kingston have brought me so much comfort during this time. When you and your husband gathered all your strength to take care of your 3 other babies, I also wanted to do the same for Penny. Car rides, extra love, more treats. Seeing them also sad is another dagger through the heart. I felt silly not going to work during Bruno's passing as I know some of my other friends who have lost pets have. I also took off yesterday and today for a long weekend to grieve and celebrate Bruno's bday. It's hard to validate to others why a "pet" deserves so much of your time and energy. But why not? They give you so much in the short amount of time they are here on this earth. They deserve days where they are remembered with tears, smiles, and heartfelt posts. Maybe there are more people out there like us but are possibly ashamed of their emotions. You have my full support."*

The messages and conversations I had with others, like my friend Molly who shared her story with me of her experience with her pup Captain, further highlighted the need to address and support those experiencing pet loss. She shared that her family decided to have Captain transition at the veterinarian office. They were told to go to the back entrance. They walked in and apparently the back of the building is also where you go for dog boarding or the salon. A chipper employee said, "oh are you here for boarding" she said no holding back tears. Employee said, "oh yes then salon is right over there." To which she screamed "I'm here to put my dog down!" through tears. Can you imagine? It's a stark reminder of how understanding and support can get needlessly fumbled and cause emotional distress in these situations. These moments could be gentler by bringing awareness, training, and establishing simple protocols like having a communication to the employees working the hour a scheduled euthanasia is taking place.

These stories, along with countless other conversations I've had, have illuminated the urgent need to normalize discussions around pet grief. There is often shame or judgment associated with feeling such profound loss for a pet. However, the truth is that the pain of losing a beloved pet can be incredibly deep and overwhelming. Their presence in our lives is filled with unconditional love, and their absence leaves an incredible void.

We need to normalize and talk more about the grief that comes with losing a pet. There is shame today that it shouldn't hurt this much. "It's just a dog" but the truth is that it hurts. I read:

"Losing A Dog Is Like Losing A Child: Most people who lose a dog will be quick to tell you that it's just like losing a child. But it's much more complicated than that. First of all, most parents will go through life without ever losing a child. When they do, they will be quick to tell you it's not supposed to be that way. But when we bring a dog into our life, it goes without saying that one day we will face losing them. In the bigger world outside the dog world, many people believe that it's "just a dog." Some believe the comparison should not be made. But in reality, everywhere in the world today, there are millions of people suffering grief that is nearly unbearable, because of the loss of a dog. Because dogs have a way of crawling into a part of our heart where we would never trust any human to go. And then, once in a while, there is that special dog who touches our soul, then leaves us with an understanding of love that surpasses all other." Beautiful words shared by Zoe the Happy Dog and @jake_the_american_bulldog on Instagram.

I felt the deep profoundness in the sentence "Because dogs have a way of crawling into a part of our heart where we would never trust any human to go."

It is important that we open dialogue and provide support for those experiencing pet loss, as well as for those who are supporting someone going through grief. This includes veterinary offices and places of employment, where sensitivity and understanding are vital during these difficult moments. By acknowledging the profound impact that pets have on our lives and promoting compassionate conversations around pet loss, we can help each other through such intense grief.

As I started this book by saying, there is understood grieving process for humans, even those we don't have the closest relationships with, but there are no ceremonies, no standard societal processes to look to for how to handle a situation for pets who are our companions. Normalizing the loss of a pet and providing support for those grieving is important. Pets are not just animals we live with; they become cherished companions, core parts of our daily lives, and sources of unconditional love and support. Yet, when they pass away, the guidance and support can feel scarce.

This disparity is surprising considering the impact they have on our lives and the depth of the bond we share with them. They become family members, and their presence shapes our routines and creates countless memories. Some even become our closest confidants, sharing our beds, and being with us through every joy and hardship. When a pet passes away, the void left behind can feel overwhelming. The grief can be unexpected and all-encompassing, as even the smallest memories can trigger intense emotions.

It is so important to validate and acknowledge the grieving process for pets. We need to create a space where people feel comfortable expressing their grief, canceling plans, and taking the time they need to heal. Grief has no timeline, and it is patient. It is essential to understand that everyone experiences it differently. Encouraging self-care and allowing individuals to prioritize their well-being, even if it means letting others down, is an important part of the healing process.

Normalizing grief in the workplace, specifically around the loss of a pet, can be incredibly meaningful. Recognizing that employees may need time off, understanding, and support during this difficult period can foster a compassionate work environment.

With only six days' notice we lost Kingston, I still know myself that regardless of how much time you get or don't get to prepare, it will never be "okay" or "easier" to go through and process. Period. The key is to allow yourself to grieve and lean on the support of loved ones, family, friends, and colleagues. Sharing our experiences, supporting one another, and normalizing pet grief can help individuals navigate their grief journey.

So, for you dear reader who has experienced pet loss or currently in it, just grieve. I hope through reading my story you feel validated in the world of hurt you are in or have experienced. It's okay to feel all the feelings. The first set of resources in Part 5 are for you. My hope is they provide some comfort in that it's okay to feel all the feelings, and also some support in how to engage with family and friends.

To those who are standing by and supporting someone facing these challenges, I want to express my heartfelt gratitude. Your willingness to acknowledge that you might not fully comprehend the depth of this experience, but are eager to understand, is a testament to your compassion and empathy. It's truly remarkable to put yourselves in someone else's shoes. The second section of Part 5 is dedicated to you. I've assembled resources to aid you in supporting a friend or family member navigating pet loss. These materials extend beyond my personal story, offering insights into their emotions. Additionally, I've shared non-material ways to extend your support, as well as suggestions for thoughtful gestures that can convey your care if you choose to do so.

To all of you who have joined me on this journey, let's stand together as advocates for change. The third section of Part 5 is dedicated materials aimed at promoting the inclusion of pets in our workplace bereavement policies. By fostering an environment that recognizes the profound impact of losing a pet and by implementing policies that provide support, we can help pet parents navigate their grief with understanding and compassion. If your organization already offers pet bereavement leave or you've been successful in adding it, I would be thrilled to hear from you. Feel free to reach out via email or connect with me on social media. Your stories inspire and drive this mission forward.

A Letter of Love to You

In closing, I want to express my deepest gratitude for allowing me to share my story and insights with you. As I reach the end of this book, I am filled with a profound sense of appreciation and hope. Through these pages, I have sought to convey the importance of love, sensitivity, and understanding in our lives.

I have shared my own experiences, vulnerabilities, and lessons learned, not as a definitive guide, but as a humble messenger of the power of empathy and connection. The tools and perspectives discussed throughout this book are not my own creations, but rather the culmination of collective wisdom, shared experiences, and conversations.

It is my heartfelt belief that by embracing love without judgment, by validating our own emotions and those of others, and by leaning on and supporting each other, we can create a more compassionate world. Each one of us has the ability to make a difference, however small, through acts of kindness and understanding.

As you journey forward, I encourage you to consider the perspectives of others, to offer grace and kindness in all your interactions, and to remember that you are enough, just as you are. Validate yourself, validate others, and cherish the connections that bring meaning and joy to your life.

Thank you for being a part of this journey. May you find the strength, courage, and love to navigate life's challenges, and may your heart be filled with compassion, understanding, and deep appreciation for the beauty of the human experience.

I will forever be grateful to Kingston. His presence in my life, albeit too brief, has left a remarkable imprint on my heart. Through his departure, he has gifted me with the opportunity to experience the depths of love and the strength to endure the pain that accompanies it. I thank him for inspiring me to embark on this journey of vulnerability and courage. Writing this book, sharing my story, and releasing it into the world was no easy feat. But Kingston's unwavering love and his transformative impact on my life have propelled me forward, pushing me to be brave, to be vulnerable, and to connect with others more deeply.

This book is my offering, my attempt to extend a helping hand to those who may be traversing their own path of loss and grief. I share my experiences, insights, and the wisdom gained from my own journey, in the hope that it may provide comfort and guidance to someone else who is grappling with the pain of loss.

Kingston, my dear son, you have gifted me a treasure beyond any measure. I am eternally grateful for the love we shared, for the lessons learned, and for the strength you've instilled within me. Your memory will forever be etched in my heart, and your spirit will continue to guide me as I strive to make a positive impact in the lives of others.

Thank you, Kingston, for the immeasurable gift of love, and for giving me the courage to share that love with the world.

Forever in my heart,

Erika

(Kingston on a Mommy and me day)

(Our 2023 family photo. We know he is still with us.)

P.S. Edmond was declared cancer-free on July 21st at the University of Illinois. We beat it. He beat it.

He showed remarkable strength throughout radiation, immunotherapies, and surgeries, and I believe Kingston was by his side all along. We now have check-ups every 4 weeks for six months, followed by check-ups every 5 weeks, in addition to immunotherapy every 6 months for the rest of his life. This aggressive cancer demands swift treatment, but Edmond is a fighter, and we're grateful we get to keep him.

PART 5:

RESOURCES

PET PARENT SUPPORT:
Navigating Grief and Preparation

- Coping with Loss
- Communication Support in personal and professional life
- A Pet Parent's Guide to Navigating the Euthanasia Discussion with Your Vet

COPING WITH LOSS

Intense grief over the loss of a pet is normal.

An inevitable aspect of bringing a companion animal into your home — a part many people rarely discuss — is the loss of a pet. When you lose your best friend, the one you could always count on when you were down, the one who warmed you, played with you and made you laugh no matter how bad you felt — it can be a devastating experience. It's important to grieve this loss and work through the emotions.[1]

People grieve the loss of a pet in different ways. Most people will experience the seven stages of grief (shock, denial, bargaining, anger, guilt, sorrow and acceptance), but the amount of time spent in each stage may vary greatly.[1]

The loss of a pet is often just as difficult, if not more so, than losing a human family member. Our relationships with animals are remarkably intimate and mutually supportive, as they love us 'no strings attached,' hold our secrets, and accept us 'just as we are.' When our daily routines include pets, the loss can be profoundly disruptive to our sense of home, sense of safety, sense of purpose, and sense of identity.[2]

What is grief like?[2]

Many are surprised by the intensity of grief anticipating and following the loss of a pet. Each person experiences grief in a different way. Children grieve just as intensely as adults do, but often have different ways of expressing their grief.

Contrary to popular belief, grief does not unfold in clean, linear stages, nor does it have a timeline. There is no absolute pattern for grief. Your experience of grief will depend on a variety of factors including your personality, your upbringing, the type of relationship you had with your pet, your personal situation at the time of your pet's death, the circumstances of the death, and your cultural and religious beliefs. Your reactions may be different from those of another pet owner, or even from those of other members of your household.

> *"Grief is a full body experience that includes physical, emotional, cognitive, social, and spiritual responses."*[2]

Socially, you may want to withdraw from others, isolating yourself from your friends, loved ones, and social circles; or oppositely, you may want to reach out to others, seeking support. You may feel like you no longer fit in with your pet-loving friends and may avoid situations where people might ask about your pet. You may use social events or work to avoid going home. There are even spiritual manifestations of grief, which include anger at, or bargaining with, a higher power; questioning of faith; searching for meaning; and wondering what happens after death ("Is my pet okay?", "Where is my pet now?", "Do animals have souls?")

These reactions are normal, healthy parts of the grief process, but can be difficult to describe to others. This can be especially true when sharing with people who do not have pets. It may be difficult for them to understand your feelings of loss. Remember, it is as perfectly normal to grieve over the loss of a beloved pet as it is over the loss of a beloved person.

What can I do to manage my grief?[2]

The best way to manage your grief is to be reassured that these reactions are normal and to let them run their natural course. Be kind to yourself as you prepare for the 'new normal' of a life without your beloved pet. Just as it took time to build the relationship with your pet, it will take time to get used to your pet not being there.

> *"A healthy grief journey comes from taking your time to work through your feelings ..."*[2]

Receive support from others. Spend time with supportive family, friends, and co-workers who understand, who will listen to your stories and feelings without judgment. Talking with others can help you come to terms with your loss. Consider joining a pet loss support group, in your locale or on-line, to help you work through your loss.

Read books on pet loss. These are published regularly and include stories of others' experiences.

Allow yourself a small break from the sadness every day. Find a source of light within the dark. Laughter serves as a healing salve for the heart, and music can soothe the soul, enabling you to cope with, and work through, your grief.

When will I get over this?[2]

It is common for people to want to feel better and 'be done with the pain.' Keep in mind that grief is not something we get over, but something we move through. When we lose someone, whose presence changed us (often for the better), we cannot help but be changed by that loss. The process of coming to terms with a loss can take a long time, but you will eventually find your way to a place where the pain of absence is less of a focus than the happy, loving memories that come to mind when you remember your pet.

Grieving takes time. It is a process, not an event. There is no specific time frame for it. In fact, grief may last for weeks, months, even years. Healthy grief, however, gradually lessens in intensity over time.

"Grieving takes time. It is a process, not an event."[2]

Remember...[2]

Remember, the experience of loss is different for everyone. It is only by moving toward the loss that one can learn to live with it. And when it comes to grief, there is no such thing as 'closure.' Although you will get through the grief, and return to a usual way of life, there may always be moments, among the happy memories, of sadness and longing. This is just a reflection of the enduring love for your pet. Although your time together ended, the love will never end.[2]

The death of a beloved pet is excruciating. With their shorter lifespans, it's also, unfortunately, an inevitability.[3]

"There's hardly a week that goes by where someone doesn't say, 'I was close to my family. When my parents died, it

was terrible. But I've never felt a loss like this,'" she said. - Therapist Susan Anschuetz, LMFT, co-founder of the Denver-based nonprofit Human Animal Bond Trust, has led free weekly pet loss support groups for more than 30 years.[3]

Ten Tips on Coping with Pet Loss[4]

1. Am I crazy to hurt so much?[4]

Intense grief over the loss of a pet is normal and natural. Don't let anyone tell you that it's silly, crazy, or overly sentimental to grieve! During the years you spent with your pet (even if they were few), it became a significant and constant part of your life. It was a source of comfort and companionship, of unconditional love and acceptance, of fun and joy. So don't be surprised if you feel devastated by the loss of such a relationship. People who don't understand the pet/owner bond may not understand your pain. All that matters, however, is how you feel. Don't let others dictate your feelings: They are valid- and may be extremely painful. But remember, you are not alone: Thousands of pet owners have gone through the same feelings.

2. What Can I Expect to Feel?[4]

Different people experience grief in different ways. Besides your sorrow and loss, you may also experience the following emotions:

- Denial makes it difficult to accept that your pet is really gone. It's hard to imagine that your pet won't greet you when you come home, or that it doesn't need its evening meal. Some pet owners carry this to extremes, and fear their pet is still alive and suffering somewhere. Others find it hard to get a new pet for fear of being "disloyal" to the old.
- Anger may be directed at the illness that killed your pet, the driver of the speeding car, the veterinarian who "failed" to save its life. Sometimes it is justified, but when carried to extremes, it distracts you from the important task of resolving your grief.

- Depression is a natural consequence of grief but can leave you powerless to cope with your feelings. Extreme depression robs you of motivation and energy, causing you to dwell upon your sorrow.

3. What can I do about my feelings?[4]

- The most important step you can take is to be honest about your feelings. Don't deny your pain, or your feelings of anger and guilt. Only by examining and coming to terms with your feelings can you begin to work through them.
- You have a right to feel pain and grief! Someone you loved has died, and you feel alone and bereaved. You have a right to feel anger and guilt, as well. Acknowledge your feelings first, then ask yourself whether the circumstances actually justify them.
- Locking away grief doesn't make it go away. Express it. Cry, scream, pound the floor, talk it out. Do what helps you the most. Don't try to avoid grief by not thinking about your pet; instead, reminisce about the good times. This will help you understand what your pet's loss actually means to you.
- Some find it helpful to express their feelings and memories in poems, stories, or letters to the pet. Other strategies including rearranging your schedule to fill in the times you would have spent with your pet; preparing a memorial such as a photo collage; and talking to others about your loss.

4. Who can I talk to?[4]

If your family or friends love pets, they'll understand what you're going through. Don't hide your feelings in a misguided effort to appear strong and calm! Working through your feelings with another person is one of the best ways to put them in perspective and find ways to handle them. Find someone you can talk to about how much the pet meant to you and how much you miss it-someone you feel comfortable crying and grieving with. If you don't have family or friends who understand, or if you need more help, ask your veterinarian or humane association to recommend a pet loss counselor or support group. Check with your church or hospital for grief counseling. Remember, your grief is genuine and deserving of support.

5. When is the right time to euthanize a pet?[4]

Your veterinarian is the best judge of your pet's physical condition; however, you are the best judge of the quality of your pet's daily life. If a pet has a good appetite, responds to attention, seeks its owner's company, and participates in play or family life, many owners feel that this is not the time. However, if a pet is in constant pain, undergoing difficult and stressful treatments that aren't helping greatly, unresponsive to affection, unaware of its surroundings, and uninterested in life, a caring pet owner will probably choose to end the beloved companion's suffering. Evaluate your pet's health honestly and unselfishly with your veterinarian. Prolonging a pet's suffering in order to prevent your own ultimately helps neither of you. Nothing can make this decision an easy or painless one, but it is truly the final act of love that you can make for your pet.

6. Should I stay during euthanasia?[4]

Many feel this is the ultimate gesture of love and comfort you can offer your pet. Some feel relief and comfort themselves by staying: They were able to see that their pet passed peacefully and without pain, and that it was truly gone. For many, not witnessing the death (and not seeing the body) makes it more difficult to accept that the pet is really gone. However, this can be traumatic, and you must ask yourself honestly whether you will be able to handle it. Uncontrolled emotions and tears-though natural-are likely to upset your pet. Some clinics are more open than others to allowing the owner to stay during euthanasia. Some veterinarians are also willing to euthanize a pet at home. Others have come to an owner's car to administer the injection. Again, consider what will be least traumatic for you and your pet, and discuss your desires and concerns with your veterinarian. If your clinic is not able to accommodate your wishes, request a referral.

7. What do I do next? [4]

When a pet dies, you must choose how to handle its remains. Sometimes, in the midst of grief, it may seem easiest to leave the pet at the clinic for disposal. Check with your clinic to find out whether there is a fee for such disposal. Some shelters also accept such remains, though many charge a fee for disposal. If you prefer a more formal option, several are available. Home burial is a popular choice if you have sufficient property for it. It is economical and enables you to design your own funeral ceremony at little cost. However, city regulations usually prohibit pet burials, and this is not a good choice for renters or people who move frequently. To many, a pet cemetery provides a sense of dignity, security, and permanence. Owners appreciate the serene surroundings and care of the gravesite. Cemetery costs vary depending on the services you select, as well as upon the type of pet you have. Cremation is a less expensive option that allows you to handle your pet's remains in a variety of ways: bury them (even in the city), scatter them in a favorite location, place them in a columbarium, or even keep them with you in a decorative urn (of which a wide variety are available). Check with your veterinarian, pet shop, or phone directory for options available in your area. Consider your living situation, personal and religious values, finances, and future plans when making your decision. It's also wise to make such plans in advance, rather than hurriedly in the midst of grief.

8. What should I tell my children? [4]

You are the best judge of how much information your children can handle about death and the loss of their pet. Don't underestimate them, however. You may find that, by being honest with them about your pet's loss, you may be able to address some fears and misperceptions they have about death. Honesty is important. If you say the pet was "put to sleep," make sure your children understand the difference between death and ordinary sleep. Never say the pet "went away," or your child may wonder what he or she did to make it leave and wait in anguish for its return. That also makes it harder for a child to accept a new pet. Make it clear that the pet will not come back, but that it is happy and free of pain. Never assume a child is too young or too old to grieve. Never criticize a child for tears or tell them to "be strong" or not to feel sad. Be honest about your own sorrow; don't try to hide it, or children may feel required to hide their grief as well. Discuss the issue with the entire family and give everyone a chance to work through their grief at their own pace.

9. Will my other pets grieve?[4]

Pets observe every change in a household and are bound to notice the absence of a companion. Pets often form strong attachments to one another, and the survivor of such a pair may seem to grieve for its companion. Cats grieve for dogs, and dogs for cats. You may need to give your surviving pets a lot of extra attention and love to help them through this period. Remember that, if you are going to introduce a new pet, your surviving pets may not accept the newcomer right away, but new bonds will grow in time. Meanwhile, the love of your surviving pets can be wonderfully healing for your own grief.

10. Should I get a new pet right away?[4]

Generally, the answer is no. One needs time to work through grief and loss before attempting to build a relationship with a new pet. If your emotions are still in turmoil, you may resent a new pet for trying to "take the place" of the old-for what you really want is your old pet back. Children in particular may feel that loving a new pet is "disloyal" to the previous pet. When you do get a new pet, avoid getting a "lookalike" pet, which makes comparisons even more likely. Don't expect your new pet to be "just like" the one you lost but allow it to develop its own personality. Never give a new pet the same name or nickname as the old. Avoid the temptation to compare the new pet to the old one: It can be hard to remember that your beloved companion also caused a few problems when it was young! A new pet should be acquired because you are ready to move forward and build a new relationship-rather than looking backward and mourning your loss. When you are ready, select an animal with whom you can build another long, loving relationship-because this is what having a pet is all about.

Losing a pet hurts—really, really hurts. And it can be hard to share that pain with others, because we humans often aren't as comfortable talking about grieving a pet as we are discussing grief for the other important friends and family in our lives. So how do you grieve a pet who's passed away? The answer, says E.B. Bartels, author of "Good Grief: On Loving Pets Here and Hereafter," is as unique and personal as your relationship with the pet who's gone.[5]

That can leave some pet parents feeling lost and confused when their pet is gone—but it also gives pet parents the freedom to choose the most fitting way to honor their beloved friend.[5]

Try to let yourself feel[6]

- You've experienced a loss, and it's OK to let yourself feel all the feelings surrounding it.
- "Cry whenever you feel like crying," says Geipert. However, she recommends using your judgment on when and where that's appropriate.
- "Tears release stress hormones." She adds that if you're not a heavy crier, that's OK too. "Everybody's way is different."

Try to practice self-compassion[6]

- Be good to yourself. Try to engage in some self-care activities as you're going through the grieving process. You can do this by making some extra space for your regular self-care activities or trying something new that you think could feel restorative.
- Take some time off from work if you need to.

Consider talking with someone who can relate[6]

- "Talking about exactly how you feel is incredibly helpful in grief, which is why it's helpful for people to go to therapy or find a support group," says Geipert.
- She recommends finding a way to talk about what and how you're feeling. You can do that with others who have lost a pet, a therapist, or supportive friends and family.
- I belonged to a disabled rabbit community and an adventure cat community online. The members were extremely supportive when I posted about losing a pet.

Try a mourning process[6]

- Societies and cultures throughout human history have engaged in mourning rituals to cope with emotional pain after a loss. Trying a ritual could also help you grieve after the death of a pet. You might try something familiar, such as having a memorial, or you could create your own practice.
- "Light a candle…honoring the anniversary of a loved one's passing"
- Geipert says she did an exercise that really helped after losing her cat. She wrote to him.
- "Write a thank-you card to your deceased pet," Geipert says. "Talk about everything you'll miss and what you're most grateful for. Talk about what you regret. Say everything you want to say."

Remove items at your own pace[6]

- Some people may want to get rid of their pet's things quickly after a loss, and others may need to do it more gradually.
- If it feels challenging to let go of your pet's items, let yourself do it at a pace that feels good for you.
- Remember that there's no right or wrong way. This is your process.

- "If you've lost your [pet] and you're completely heartbroken, know that that's a sign of how mentally healthy you are," says Geipert. "You have the capacity for deep love; it's a good thing."

Other ways people can deal with their emotions and practice self-kindness while mourning the loss of a pet include[7]:

- Having a memorial service or funeral. Some people may choose to bury a pet or spread their ashes in their favorite place. This can help people get a better sense of closure.
- Reflecting on positive memories by making a list, writing a letter, or choosing a picture to frame and hang in the home.
- Spending some time in the pet's favorite places. This may include going to a dog park, taking a walk down a familiar route, or even just spending some time in the yard.

If your emotions are very strong and you're having a hard time dealing with them, you can consider going to individual or group therapy. Therapists can help people better identify their emotions and learn to work through them to get to a healthier place. This is especially important for people who experience symptoms of anxiety or depression following loss of a pet.[7]

Pet Loss Support Phone Hotlines[8]

National Resources

- Tufts University Pet Loss Support Hotline– 508-839-7966
- Chicago Veterinary Medical Association Support Line – 630-325-1600
- Cornell University Pet Loss Support Hotline – 607-218-7457

Local Resources

For local and regional phone hotlines, check with your local Veterinary Colleges and Humane Societies.

Support Groups[8]

Virtual Support Group

- Lap of Love Pet Loss Support Group

Individual Counseling[8]

You can also search the internet for grief or pet loss counselors in your area. If you find a grief counselor, reach out and ask if they are comfortable with counseling for pet loss.

Books for Adults

- *When Your Pet Dies: A Guide to Mourning, Remembering and Healing* by Alan Wolfelt[8]
- *Pet Loss: A Thoughtful Guide for Adults and Children* by Herbert Neiburg and Arlene Fischer[8]
- *Goodbye My Friend: Grieving the Loss of a Pet* by Mary and Herb Montgomery[8]
- *The Loss of a Pet* by Wallace Sife[8]
- *Saying Goodbye to the Pet You Love* by Lorri Greene[8]
- *The Grief Recovery Handbook for Pet Loss* by Russell Friedman[8]
- *Coping With Sorrow on the Loss of Your Pet* by Moira Anderson Allen[8]
- *Coping With the Loss of Your Pet* by Christine Lemieux[8]
- *My Personal Pet Remembrance Journal* by Enid Samuel Traisman[8]
- *Pet Parents: A Journey Through Unconditional Love and Grief* by Coleen Ellis[8]

Books for Children[8]

- *When a Pet Dies* by Fred Rogers
- *The Tenth Good Thing About Barney* by Judith Viorst
- *Dog Heaven* by Cynthia Rylant
- *Cat Heaven* by Cynthia Rylant
- *I'll Always Love You* by Hans Wilhelm
- *Healing Your Grieving Heart for Kids* by Alan Wolfeldt

- *Saying Goodbye to Lulu by Corinne Demas*
- *Goodbye Mousie* by Robbie Harris
- *The Fall of Freddie the Leaf* by Leo Buscaglia
- *Forever Friend: A children's guide and activity book for saying goodbye to a special dog* by Mary Gardner and Coleen Ellis *Forever Friend: A children's guide and activity book for saying goodbye to a special cat* by Mary Gardner and Coleen Ellis

References

1. *Pet Loss & Grief - American Humane.* (2023, May 16). American Humane. Retrieved June 17, 2023, from https://www.americanhumane.org/fact-sheet/pet-loss-grief/
2. Hunter, T. H., DVM, & Stoewen, D., DVM, MSW, RSW, PhD. (2023). *Loss of a Pet - Grief and Bereavement | VCA Animal Hospitals.* www.VCAHospitals.com. Retrieved June 17, 2023, from https://vcahospitals.com/know-your-pet/grief-and-bereavement—-loss-of-a-pet
3. Reeder, Jen. "Why the Loss of a Pet Is So Challenging & Tips for Coping With Grief." *Www.Fearfreehappyhomes.Com*, 19 May 2021, Why the Loss of a Pet Is So Challenging & Tips for Coping With Grief. Accessed 11 Jun. 2023.
4. Anderson Allen, M., M. Ed. (2023). *Ten Tips on Coping with Pet Loss.* www.homwithdignity.com. Retrieved June 17, 2023, from https://homewithdignity.com/ten-tips-on-coping-with-pet-loss/
5. Sparacino, A. (2023). How Do You Mourn the Loss of a Pet? Any Way You Want, Says "Good Grief" Author E.B. Bartels. *BeChewy.* https://be.chewy.com/loss-of-a-pet-good-grief-author-e-b-bartels-interview/?gbraid=123&utm_source=google&utm_medium=cpc&utm_campaign=12473032557&utm_content=118814524259&gbraid=0AAAADmQ2V0m_tX6jiDkeBo7WFxRp3O-Hy&gclid=EAIaIQobChMIsvmEv8G3_wIVlQmzAB0jzwJREAMYASAAEgJGKPD_BwE
6. Goldman, R. (2021, October 14). *How to Cope When You're Grieving the Loss of a Pet.* Psych Central. Retrieved June 17, 2023, from https://psychcentral.com/lib/grieving-the-loss-of-a-pet#why-its-painful
7. Connor, B., MD. (2021c, February 26). *Grieving the Loss of a Pet - Brynna Connor MD.* Brynna Connor MD. Retrieved June 17, 2023, from https://doctorconnor.com/grieving-the-loss-of-a-pet/#:~:text=Pet%20Loss%20and%20Mental%20Health&text=Some%20people%20experience%20mental%20symptoms,and%20depression%20for%20some%20people.
8. *Pet Loss Resources - Companion Animal Euthanasia Training Academy.* (2022, December 7). CAETA. Retrieved June 17, 2023, from https://caetainternational.com/about/caeta-pet-loss-resources/

COMMUNICATION SUPPORT PERSONALLY AND AT WORK

6 TEXTS YOU COULD SEND WHEN SOMEONE ASKS YOU TO DO SOMETHING YOU DON'T WANT TO DO

- "I can't make it. I'm going through a tough time right now."
- "Thank you so much for thinking of me! I truly appreciate your invitation, but at the moment, I'm going through a difficult time. I hope you understand and that we can catch up soon when I'm feeling a bit better."
- "I'm not up for it. Can we do something another time?"
- "I want to be honest with you and share that I'm currently navigating a period of grief, and it's been challenging for me to engage in social activities. Can we reschedule to a later date when I'm in a better emotional space? Your understanding means a lot to me."
- Sorry, but I'm just not interested in doing that right now."
- "Thank you for considering me for this, but I must admit that I'm going through a grieving process, which makes it challenging for me to participate in certain activities. I hope you can understand my need to take some time for self-care and healing."
- "Thanks for thinking of me! I really appreciate the invitation. However, I'm not really into that genre of music, and lately, I've been feeling a bit overwhelmed with everything going on. I think I need a more relaxed environment for now. Let's plan something else together soon, though!"
- "I love that you're into hiking, and it sounds like a fantastic plan! But I feel the need to take some quiet time for myself this weekend to reflect and recharge. I hope you understand, and maybe we can go hiking together another time or find something else fun to do together soon"

- "Thanks for inviting me to the party! I truly appreciate it. However, I'm going through a difficult time, and I'm finding social gatherings a bit challenging at the moment. I hope you have a blast at the party, and maybe we can catch up one-on-one sometime soon."
- "It's so thoughtful of you to invite me to the movie! I've heard good things about it, but I must admit it's not quite my cup of tea. However, I'd love to see you and hang out. How about we pick another movie or activity that we both enjoy? I'm sure it'll be a fantastic time together!"

3 TEXTS TO SEND WHEN YOU'VE CHANGED YOUR MIND

Changing your mind is completely normal, and it's important to communicate it respectfully. Here are three texts you could send to let someone know you've changed your mind about a commitment:

- "Hey [Friend's Name], I hope you're doing well. I wanted to talk to you about our previous plans. After some careful consideration, I realized that I need to change my decision. I hope you understand that circumstances have shifted, and I hope we can find another time to connect. Thanks for being understanding."
- "Hi [Friend's Name], I hope you're having a great day. I wanted to reach out and be honest with you. I need to change my plans. I know this might be unexpected, but I hope you can appreciate my honesty. Let's chat and figure out a better time to catch up."
- "Dear [Friend's Name], I hope this message finds you well. I wanted to talk to you about the commitment I made earlier. I've given it much thought, and I believe it's best if I change my mind. I hope you understand that sometimes situations change, and I value our friendship enough to be upfront about it. Let's talk soon and find a resolution that works for both of us."

Remember, it's crucial to be considerate and respectful when communicating changes in plans. Friends who care about you will appreciate your honesty and understanding that life can be unpredictable.

TEXT REPLIES WHEN SOMEONE CALLS YOU, BUT YOU DON'T HAVE THE ENERGY

When you're feeling low on energy and someone wants to talk, it's essential to respond thoughtfully and honestly while still being considerate of their feelings. Here are four text replies you could use:

- "Hey [Friend's Name], thanks for reaching out. I really appreciate your desire to talk, but I'm currently feeling quite drained and low on energy. Can we catch up tomorrow or later in the week when I'll be in a better headspace? I hope you understand."
- "Hi there, I hope you're doing well. I wanted to be honest with you; I'm feeling emotionally exhausted today and don't think I can give our conversation the attention it deserves. Can we reschedule for when I'm feeling more refreshed? Thank you for your understanding."
- "Thanks for thinking of me. I wish I could chat right now, but I'm running on fumes today and need to take some time to recharge. Can we talk tomorrow morning when I'll be more alert and able to engage in a meaningful conversation?"
- "Hey, I'm grateful you reached out, but I'm feeling quite depleted at the moment. My energy levels are low, and I wouldn't want our conversation to suffer because of it. Can we connect later when I've had a chance to rest? Thanks for your understanding."

Remember, it's okay to prioritize self-care and set boundaries when you need time to recharge. Your friends will appreciate your honesty, and genuine connections can still be maintained even if you need some space occasionally.

3 TEXTS YOU COULD SEND WHEN SOMEONE ASKS YOU TO DO SOMETHING YOU DON'T WANT TO DO

Here are four text replies you could use when someone asks you to do something you don't want to do:

- "Hi there, I hope you're doing well. I wanted to let you know that I'm not really up for [the requested activity] at the moment. I'm trying to focus on other priorities right now, but I appreciate the offer. Let's plan something else that suits both of us better when we have the chance!"
- "Thanks for the invite! I genuinely value our friendship, but I'm going through a bit of a busy period right now, and I won't be able to join in. I hope you have a fantastic time, and let's catch up soon for coffee or a less time-consuming activity!"
- "Hey, I'm grateful you asked, but I have to decline this time. It's not something I'm interested in or comfortable doing. I hope you have a wonderful experience, and I look forward to hanging out under different circumstances!"

Remember, being honest yet considerate in your replies is essential. Your friends will appreciate your openness, and it shows that you value your relationship enough to communicate your feelings sincerely.

3 TEXTS TO HELP YOU ASK FOR WHAT YOU NEED

- Hi [Recipient's Name], I hope you're doing well. I was hoping to talk to you about something important to me. I need some assistance with [specific task or favor] and was wondering if you could lend a hand. It would mean a lot to me. Let me know if you're available to chat or help. Thanks!"
- "Hey [Recipient's Name], I wanted to reach out and discuss my current situation. I could really use some advice or guidance on [the issue or topic]. I know you have experience in this area, and your insights would be incredibly valuable to me. If you have a moment, I'd be grateful to have a conversation with you. Thanks for being there for me!"

- "Dear [Recipient's Name], I hope this message finds you well. I'm going through a tough time, and I'm realizing that I need some emotional support right now. Would you be available to talk or meet up sometime soon? Your friendship means a lot to me, and having someone to lean on during difficult moments would be incredibly comforting. Let me know if you're available. Thanks for listening."

Asking for what you need can be challenging, but being open and straightforward in your communication can lead to more understanding and supportive relationships. Don't hesitate to reach out when you require help, advice, or emotional support; true friends will be there for you when you need them.

EMAILS YOU COULD SEND TO COMMUNICATE BOUNDARIES AT WORK

When returning from bereavement leave, it's essential to communicate your boundaries with sensitivity and request support during the transition. Here are two email examples from the perspective of someone coming back from bereavement leave:

Email 1: Setting Priorities and Requesting Grace

To: Your Manager

Subject: Re: New project and Returning from Bereavement Leave

Dear [Manager's Name],

I hope this email finds you well. First and foremost, I want to express my gratitude for the support and understanding you've shown during my bereavement leave. It meant a lot to me during this challenging time.

As I transition back to work, I wanted to be open about my current state. Grieving the loss of [Name] has been emotionally taxing, and I'm still adjusting to the return to the workplace.

Regarding the new project you assigned, I want to ensure that I can give it the attention it deserves while managing my well-being. Could we discuss the priority of this project and how we can manage my workload to avoid overwhelming me during this period?

I understand the importance of the project and my responsibilities, but I would appreciate some grace as I find my footing again. If possible, I'd like to gradually ease back into full capacity to ensure I can maintain my focus and meet expectations effectively.

Thank you for your understanding and support during this time. I look forward to discussing this further with you and working together to create a plan that benefits both the project and my well-being.

Warm regards,

[Your Name]

Email 2: Establishing Boundaries for Overtime and Requesting Flexibility

To: Your Manager

Subject: Overtime Request and Returning from Bereavement Leave

Dear [Manager's Name],

I hope you are doing well. I wanted to discuss the request to work overtime on the upcoming project now that I've returned from my bereavement leave.

I deeply appreciate the consideration and support you've shown me during this challenging time, and I'm eager to contribute effectively to the team. However, I must also be honest about my current capacity.

Grieving the loss of [Name] has taken an emotional toll, and I want to prioritize my well-being as I transition back to work. While I'm committed to fulfilling my responsibilities, I may need some flexibility when it comes to overtime.

If the situation requires immediate attention, I'll do my best to support the team. However, I would be grateful if we could collaborate on a plan that ensures a manageable workload and avoids prolonged overtime during this period.

Thank you for understanding the delicate balance I'm trying to maintain. Your continued support and flexibility as I navigate this transition would be immensely valuable.

Kind regards,

[Your Name]

Remember, when returning from bereavement leave, it's essential to be open about your needs while appreciating the support your employer provides. Communication with empathy can lead to a smoother reintegration into the workplace.

PHRASES TO HELP YOU "PAUSE BEFORE YOU RESPOND TO INVITES + REQUESTS

Taking a moment to pause and carefully consider your response to invites and requests can lead to more thoughtful and informed decisions. Here are five phrases to help you in those situations:

- "Thank you for the invitation/request. Let me check my schedule and get back to you shortly."
- "I appreciate you thinking of me. Before I commit, I need to see if I have any prior commitments on that day. I'll get back to you as soon as possible."
- "I'm honored you asked me. However, I'd like to take a moment to think it over and make sure I can give it my full attention. Can I respond to you by [specific date]?"

- "That sounds interesting, but I need some time to consider whether it aligns with my current priorities and responsibilities. Is it alright if I let you know tomorrow?"
- "Thanks for reaching out. I want to give your request the consideration it deserves, so I'll take a little time to think about it and give you a well-thought-out response."

Taking a moment to pause before responding allows you to avoid making hasty decisions and ensures that your commitments align with your current goals and priorities. It's okay to take your time and give yourself the space to make informed choices.

A Pet Parent's Guide to Navigating the Euthanasia Discussion with Your Vet

Dear fellow pet parents, I understand the immense pain and heartache that comes with the decision to euthanize. It's an emotional journey, and I want to help you navigate this difficult conversation with your veterinarian. I hope my experiences can guide you in case your vet practice doesn't have refined protocols for this sensitive topic. Remember, you are not alone in this journey, and seeking support is crucial during this time.

Step 1: Opening Up About Your Feelings and Concerns

When discussing euthanasia with your vet, it's important to express your feelings and concerns openly. Don't hold back or feel like you're burdening them. Your vet cares about your pet and your emotional well-being. Share your fears, doubts, and emotions, knowing that they will listen with compassion and understanding. They may not have experienced the same bond you share with your pet, but they want to support you throughout this difficult process.

Step 2: Understanding the Euthanasia Process Together

If your vet practice doesn't have a predefined process for discussing euthanasia, it's essential to take the lead and ask questions. Inquire about the method of euthanasia, what to expect during the procedure, and whether sedation will be provided to ensure your pet's comfort. Remember, your veterinarian is there to guide you, and you deserve clarity and empathy during this challenging time.

Step 3: Pre-planning and Aftercare Decisions

Initiate a conversation about pre-planning with your veterinarian to make the process smoother. Discuss keeping your pet's leash, getting a paw print, or selecting an urn for their ashes. This proactive approach can help ease the burden on the day of the euthanasia. Additionally, inquire about the available aftercare options, such as individual or communal cremation, and the return of your pet's ashes if desired.

Understanding these details ahead of time can bring a sense of control amidst the grief.

Step 4: Emphasizing Your Needs and Seeking Support

Remember, this is a time for you and your pet, and it's crucial to emphasize your needs. If your vet practice isn't well-versed in discussing euthanasia, advocate for yourself and your pet's comfort. They may not know the depth of your emotional bond, so don't hesitate to share your feelings and ask for understanding and support. Reach out to friends, family, or support groups who have experienced pet loss – they can offer valuable guidance and empathy during this challenging period.

As fellow pet parents who have navigated the heartbreaking journey of euthanasia, I want to help you during this emotional time. Remember, you have the right to grieve and seek support during this difficult journey. Your pet's well-being and your emotional needs are valid and deserve the utmost care and understanding. May your precious companion find peace, and may you find comfort in knowing that you are not alone.

HOW TO SUPPORT A FRIEND OR FAMILY MEMBER GOING THROUGH PET LOSS

- Understanding how the person you care about is feeling
- Non-Material Ways to Offer Support
- Thoughtful ways to show you care

Understanding how the person you care about is feeling

Why Pet Loss Hurts[1]

One reason why losing a pet is such a deep loss is because animals' love is so unconditional and accepting. But it's also because so many aspects of people's lives are impacted. Every single facet of life is part of the loss.[1] Pet parents often say that losing their animal companions is as hard as, if not harder than, losing a human family member, experts say.[2] "Your pets follow you into bathroom. They sleep with you. They are your shadow. Human family members don't do that," said Leigh Ann Gerk, a pet loss grief counselor in Loveland, Colo., and founder of Mourning to Light Pet Loss. "Humans don't go crazy with joy when you come back inside after getting the mail. Human relationships, while important, can be difficult. Our relationship with our pets is simple. They love us just as we are."[2]

When we are caretakers for animals, it multiplies the intensity just before they die. It's like their whole life has been shredded.[1] Our pets often have seen us through major life changes, from divorce or illness to starting a new school or job, so the relationship can be devastating to lose.[1]

Although pet lovers can relate to the heartbreak, grieving the loss of a pet, as opposed to a human, is still a disenfranchised grief in today's society. Comments like "It's just a dog," or "Are you going to get another cat?" can feel hurtful and isolating. "Many who come to the group are people who had this once-in-a-lifetime special bond," Anschuetz said. "They don't want to hear about getting another pet. And they shouldn't until their grief process is done."[1]

The Added Weight of Euthanasia[1]

People in each pet loss support group discuss feelings of guilt for having to euthanize a pet. Often they are upset because they felt uncertain about when it was time to let go. It's a really heavy responsibility, but it can be such a gift to the animal.

Alternately, sometimes those who cared for an ailing pet for years feel guilty for feeling some relief at their death or having moments in which they briefly feel better.

Anschuetz, who has lost many pets herself, emphasized it is okay to not be in a constant state of grief. "Grief is so variable," she said. "Take advantage of those moments when you're feeling a little bit better and then make sure that you leave yourself time to grieve, some time every day, as long as you need to. Don't run away from it."[1]

Perhaps most importantly, remember there is no single way to grieve the loss of a pet and that you're not alone. Anschuetz said her goal is to help people move through grief to grow into a richer capacity to love, rather than diminish into a lesser capacity to love because of fear of loss and pain. "We're all in this together," she said.[1]

People want to help, but often don't know how. Sometimes their comments can hurt.

> ***"Greater society doesn't recognize the intensity of this loss and the grieving that comes with it," said Jessica Kwerel, a D.C. psychotherapist who specializes in pet loss.***[2]

How to support grieving pet parents[2]

We spoke with pet loss grief experts about how people can support grieving pet parents. Here is their advice:

- **Avoid euphemisms and platitudes.** Don't say, "They are in a better place," since "the only place you want your pet is in your home," Gerk said. Other things not to say: "They're running free," "They're not in pain anymore," "They're with your other dogs now," "They've gained their wings" or "Everything happens for a reason."
    - **It is part of God's plan.** This implies that God's plan is to cause us extreme pain.[5]
    - **At least you have your other pets to love**. I don't want my other pets. I want this pet.[5]

    - **It is time to get on with your life.** I'm not ready to move on. Now I feel even worse. [5]
    - **I know how much you loved him/her.** No, you don't how much love I had for this pet. [5]
    - **They lived a long happy life with you.** You should be happy about that. No, I'm actually very sad that they are gone. Losing a pet I love after so many years hurts.[5]
    - **With as many pets as you have, you should be used to this by now.** No, I'll never get used to the pain. Each loss brings about a new feeling of pain. [5]
- While some people might find these phrases healing, others may see them as dismissive, Kwerel said. "That's trying to apply logic to an emotional experience," she said.
- Never say an animal has been "put to sleep," when explaining a pet's death to a young child. They may fear going to sleep at night. "Instead, you can say: 'We helped him along in his dying process,'" Kwerel said.
- **Be careful with Rainbow Bridge imagery.** The Rainbow Bridge is a mythical overpass where grieving pet parents are said to reunite forever with their departed animals. "That's not a belief system for some people," Gerk said. "I've had clients say they want to believe in the Rainbow Bridge, but they don't know if they do. I remind them: if it brings them comfort to believe in it, then believe in it."
- **Provide validation with facts, if possible.** I lost one of my dogs, Raylan, recently to splenic hemangiosarcoma, an aggressive and fatal cancer. After surgery and chemotherapy, Raylan enjoyed five terrific months before the cancer returned.
    - A stranger wrote this to me via a Facebook dog rescue group: "I am a human pathologist. This kind of cancer is essentially incurable in both people and dogs. Five

months of quality time after first diagnosis is fantastic. You did the right thing, no matter how hard. Don't second guess yourself. Further efforts would have just prolonged suffering."

- Guilt often goes along with mourning, and his comments eased both for me.

- **Share your pet grief story.** It can help the grieving pet parent to know you've been through it, too, but don't make it about yourself.
  - "Don't compare grief situations," said Michele Pich, assistant director of the Shreiber Family Pet Therapy program at Rowan University. "That won't help. You can say: 'I understand how painful this can be,' but keep the focus on this current experience."
- **If you knew the pet, share your memories.** It's helpful for pet owners "to know their animal has made an impact on other people's lives as well as their own," Pich said. And use the pet's name rather than saying, "your dog" or "your cat," Gerk suggested.
- **Don't minimize the loss or try to find a silver lining.** It wasn't "just" a cat, or "just" a dog. It was a family member. And don't say, "Now you can travel," "You won't be tied down anymore," or "Your vet bills won't be so high."
- **There is no time limit on grief.** Try not to rush the process, Pich said. "Sometimes people will have sympathy for a day or two, then not understand why you are still grieving weeks or months later," she said. And don't say, "Don't cry." That puts a terrible burden on the griever. You also shouldn't predict that your friend will "get over" it. Don't tell people what to do or how they are going to feel, Kwerel said. "You're not in charge of their feelings." Pich agreed. "There won't be a time when

you don't love or miss them," she said. "It doesn't go away. It just becomes more tolerable."

- **Listen.** "Grief is not a problem to be solved," Kwerel said. "You can't take away their pain. Just be a compassionate witness to it."
- **Discourage big changes right after a pet dies.** "For example, someone might say: I drove them to the vet in this car, so I'm getting rid of the car,'" Pich said. "Let them get to a better place when they can make rational decisions."
- **Don't ask what you can do.** "That puts the onus on the griever," Kwerel said. Instead, do something concrete such as sending flowers and showing up with pizza. Say, 'I'm here for you.'" You can also send a text, email or voice message, but say no response is necessary.
- **Don't suggest getting another cat or dog without adding "when you are ready."** Pushing them implies they are replacing the one who died. Gerk said she has had clients who needed companionship right away, others never adopted again and still others adopted when they felt ready. "Some are afraid to feel that loss again," she said, "but I remind them that all those years are worth it."[2]

In times of tragic loss, many people reach out to their friends and family for sympathy, while others keep to themselves. Knowing how to support your friend during an emotional time can help them feel more at ease. With the right insight and knowledge, you can understand what type of griever they are and learn how to care for them in the best way possible.[3]

Below is a guide to help you in taking the right steps to be there for your friend, whether it's sitting down and listening or helping them find a positive outlet for their sorrows.[3]

My Friend Lost Their Pet — What Can I Do?

The key to comforting a friend who lost a pet is to be empathetic. Put yourself in their shoes, see their perspective and recognize their emotions.

1. **Understand What They're Going Through and How They May Project Grief**
    a. Your first step is to understand bereavement. Grieving isn't reserved for the loss of humans, and feeling emotionally vulnerable is natural when you lose a pet. Your friend needs to process their feelings. [3]
    b. Sometimes the loss of a pet can be overwhelming. However, your friend can cope by talking to a friend, family member or a grief counselor. They can ask about funeral arrangement support from their veterinarian or local pet crematorium. They should also have enough time to grieve according to their own terms. [3]
    c. It's imperative to understand that people mourn differently — there is not a one-size-fits-all way to support your friend. Sorrow is a natural reaction to losing something important and loved. People can grieve through physical, social, behavioral or cognitive approaches. [3]
    d. Various types of mourning can range from delayed, complicated and chronic to masked, distorted and inhibited[3]
2. **Offer if you can relieve stress (adaptation)**
    a. If you're willing to lend a hand, it can relieve a bit of stress from their life. Many times, a friend may ask you to research pet afterlife arrangements because it's a touchy subject that may cause them more emotional pain.
    b. If you're willing and able, make any afterlife preparations according to their specific requests. You also may be able

to help by completing daily tasks like grocery shopping, house cleaning or making dinner.

c. However, some people may not want hands-on support and prefer personal space. They may feel comfortable doing things themselves instead of relying on someone else. That's why it's crucial to ask what you can do instead of assuming.

Support Them Based on How They Grieve[3]

Knowing how someone deals with heartache can help you be the best support system. Studies show that people experience a significant attachment to their dogs, cats and other pets and undergo substantial stages of grief reactions.

What You Can Say

The best way to comfort someone dealing with the loss of a beloved pet is to console them in person. Always mean what you say and stick with them, whether it takes your friend a few weeks, months or years to come to terms with their loss. Simply validate their grieving and emotions.[3]

What Not to Do[3]

It's easy to feel uncomfortable when your friend is mourning the loss of their pet, but it's important not to say the wrong thing. Don't try to fix the problem, give them pep talks or offer advice. Let the process take its course and avoid using logic because it's not comforting. Guidance on what not to say includes:

- Using euphemisms
- Avoiding saying the pet's name
- Filling awkward silences
- Telling them, "It will be okay."
- Saying, "It's for the best," or, "Think of all the great memories."
- Comparing their pain to another's

- Recommending they get another pet
- Saying you understand how they feel because no one grieves the same way
- Implying that time heals all wounds
- Saying their pet is in a better place
- Comparing their pet's loss to your own experience
- Imposing a timeline of feeling better

People don't want to hear false hope or cliché sentiments. Your friend isn't looking for a replacement pet, either. They will get another when their heart is ready to move on. Supporting your friend after they lose their best fur friend is all about knowing their needs and being genuine.

References:

1. Reeder, Jen. "Why the Loss of a Pet Is So Challenging & Tips for Coping With Grief." *Www.Fearfreehappyhomes.Com*, 19 May 2021, Why the Loss of a Pet Is So Challenging & Tips for Coping With Grief. Accessed 11 Jun. 2023.
2. Cimons, Marlene. "Dealing with Pet Loss: How to Help a Grieving Pet Parent." *Www.Washingtonpost.Com*, 31 Jan. 2023, www.washingtonpost.com/wellness/2023/01/31/grief-pets-loss/. Accessed 11 Jun. 2023. 3. Hyde, Jennifer. "Dealing with Pet Loss: How to Help a Grieving Pet Parent." *Www.Agapepetservices.Com*, 26 Feb. 2020, agapepetservices.com/pet-loss-supporting-a-friend/. Accessed 11 Jun. 2023.
4. "6 Ways to Help a Friend Whose Pet Died." *Www.Thepetmemorial.Org*, 2 Feb. 2021, thepetmemorial.org/six-ways-to-help-a-friend-whose-pet-died/. Accessed 11 Jun. 2023.
5. Anderson, Karen A. *The Amazing Afterlife of Animals*. 1st ed., *Rain Publishing*, 2017. pp. 127-130.

Non-Material Ways to Offer Support

Any pet lover knows how hard it can be to process the death of a beloved pet. One of the most meaningful things you can do for a friend who recently lost their pet is to simply reach out. Let them know you're thinking of them and their pet. This simple step can make the process of healing easier for them, but you may be looking for other ways you can be there for them.[1]

If you're looking for more ways you can help your friend, here are ways you can provide comfort to a friend who lost their pet.[1]

Validate Their Feelings[1]

Let them know what they're feeling is okay and expected. Losing a pet is a difficult experience for pet owners, so let them know it's okay to feel upset.

Give Them Time[1]

In the midst of a loss, it's common to try to shed a bright light on what has happened to dampen negative emotions. Be careful not to move too fast. Again, it's okay if your friend is sad, so don't rush into positivity because it may undermine the severity of the person's loss.

Remind Them to Be Gentle With Themselves[1]

In some instances, pet owners are forced to put their pets down as they reach an old age or experience health complications. This can be difficult to come to terms with and your friend may be questioning whether they made the right decision. These feelings are understandable.

While it's important to listen, if they are saying things like "it's my fault" or "I made the wrong decision", challenge these sentiments and validate the decision they made for their pet. Don't let them blame themselves for any difficult decision they had to make for their pet while they were nearing the end of their life. Make sure they know they are a loving, caring, and responsible pet owner who always had their pet's best interests at heart.

Take a Walk With Your Friend[1]

Exercise won't cure grief, but it can help boost your mood by releasing endorphins. Going on a walk outdoors can also be a great time for the person to talk about their pet loss with you if they're comfortable. Not only will your friend be coping with a loss, but they may be readjusting to a new routine in their life without a pet to take care of. Going for walks together can help them establish a new routine after their pet has passed.

Additionally, spending time in nature can have healing effects for people experiencing grief or loss. Experiencing nature can improve wellbeing and mental health for everyone and especially for those grieving.

Check in with them in the days, weeks and months after a loss. It only takes a second, but it means a lot to that person.[1]

- Sometimes just being there with them not saying a word is helpful.
- Some people want to be alone. So text or reach out to let them know you care.

Here are some ways to support those you care about in a way that feels good to you.

In Person[2]

Several things you can say include:[2]

- "Nothing I say can make you feel better, but I'm here for you." [2]
- "I know you loved them dearly." [2]
- "They were part of your family." [2]
- ""They were lucky to have you." [2]
- "No matter what, I'll be by your side." [2]
- "Please know I'll be thinking of you." [2]
- You can also recall positive memories of their dog or cat and explain how their pet positively impacted your life — touch

on how you will miss them or any personal stories about their furry family member. [2]

In Text

Here are a few examples of what you can say when someone has suffered a loss:

- Acknowledge their loss:[3]
- "I'm so sorry to hear that (say their name) has passed away. [3]
- "I can't imagine how difficult this must be for you." [3]
- "I'm sorry you are going through this difficult time." [3]
- "I'm here for you." [3]
- "If you want to talk, I'm here."[3]
- "How are you doing?? I'm so sorry I didn't know about (pet name) - this is some serious hard times."
- "You are doing everything right. Let me know if you want to talk totally understand if not and my 🙏"
- "Thinking of you guys a lot."
- "I want to chat with you when you want to chat with a friend."
- "You are in a world of hurt."
- It's okay to share a story or something you find that reminds you of them – here is an example of one I received that brought joy. It came along with a picture of Kingston.
  - "I just happened to be looking for photos on a specific date in the past and this was there. It was meant to be that I saw these. This boy is clearly watching out for you and I think he wants me to share."
- "I know…it's horrible. And I also know you gave him such a good life. And he gave you so much. And that's the only thing that will get you all through it."
- "Just wanted to check in….hope you all are doing ok."

- "No need to respond, just sending you love (loved one's name)"
- "Just wanted to let you know I'm thinking of ALL of you, and sending you my peace xo
- "Just checking in on you."
- "Can I come visit tomorrow?"
- "I've been thinking about you guys."
- "Huge hugs to you. Let me know if you need anything. I could just sit in your living room, play guitar and tell shitty jokes while you two drink wine if it would help."
- "So sorry you are going through this. I'm here and at the ready to help."
- "You don't have to respond, I just want you to know I'm thinking of you all. Remember the law of energy... energy cannot be created nor destroyed. All his energy, every vibration, all that makes him him, cannot simply cease. It'll leave the physical form you know, but it will still be out there. It's what's able to send the signs once they transition. I was told their hearing is the last to go, so as he is transitioning, whenever that may be, whisper all the sweet everything's in his ear - tell him how brave he is, how handsome he is, that he's been the best best boy to ever be a brother to those other lucky pups of yours. Sending you all the love and light. Please give him a pat on his cute noggin for me. 😔"
- "hey (friends name) you and (if they have a partner) have been on my mind a lot lately! I've been praying for (pets name) and for your family. You are the best dog mom I know, (say pets name) is a lucky lucky (type of animal)! ❤ I love you!"
- A heart emoji
- "I just wanted to say I'm so damn sorry about (pets name)! I know words don't help but we're thinking about you guys."

- "Hey friend. I've been following your story and am so touched. Sending you love."
- "Sending you lots of love in the coming days and weeks. Grief is messy and hard."
- "I'm here if you ever need to talk."
- "Hi (loved one's name), thinking of you today. I can only imagine how tough it is. Sending all the love and prayers to your family, especially to (pets name) ♥"
- "Take it as slow as you need to: day by day, hour by hour, minute to minute, or just breath to breath, heartbeat to heartbeat. You won't ever get used to it, get over it, or find it normal. It's like losing a limb or your sight. You know what it's like to have it and you learn to adapt without it. At some point, you adapt well enough that people wouldn't know the difference, but your body always will. And that's okay. People often say stupid things when they mean well. You are not obligated to listen to anyone's condolences or advice at any point. "
- "Just know as you go out in the world it is okay to tell your (insert nail person, hair stylist) that you are going through grief and that you can't talk that day. They will respect you. You have to take care of you."

In a Card[2]

If you choose to write a sympathy card, display the same emotions and feelings of comfort as you would in-person. Sending a comforting message may feel intimidating, but your words can reach further than you expect. Even offering to help with daily tasks can ease their grief. Comforting statements you can write in a card include:

- "I've been thinking of you. How are you holding up?" [2]
- "I'm praying for you and your family." [2]
- "I'm sorry for your loss. They will be missed." [2]
- "They were lucky to have you as their owner and best friend." [2]

- "Sending loving thoughts your way." [2]
- "If you need to talk, I'm always here." [2]
- "Wishing you peace and comfort during this difficult time." [2]
- "Don't hesitate to call me." [2]
- "If you need to sit down and talk, let me know." [2]
- "Losing a part of your family is never easy."[2]

Sending a card or handwritten letter can be felt as more heartfelt and thoughtful, but reaching out in anyway will show love.

When someone you know has suffered the loss of a pet, try to be sensitive to their fragile emotions. Perhaps you can remember how you felt after you suffered a loss. Kindness goes a long way.[6]

Check in with them. It only takes a second, but it means a lot to that person.

- Sometimes just being there with them not saying a word is helpful.
- Some people want to be alone. So text or reach out to let them know you care.

References:

1. "6 Ways to Help a Friend Whose Pet Died." *Www.Thepetmemorial.Org.Com*, 2 Feb. 2021, thepetmemorial.org/six-ways-to-help-a-friend-whose-pet-died/. Accessed 11 Jun. 2023.
2. Hyde, Jennifer. "Dealing with Pet Loss: How to Help a Grieving Pet Parent." *Www.Agapepetservices.Com*, 26 Feb. 2020, agapepetservices.com/pet-loss-supporting-a-friend/. Accessed 11 Jun. 2023. TWO
3. Anderson, Karen A. *The Amazing Afterlife of Animals.* 1st ed., *Rain Publishing*, 2017. pp. 127-130.

Thoughtful Gifts to Show You Care

Any pet lover knows how hard it can be to process the death of a beloved pet. One of the most meaningful things you can do for a friend who recently lost their pet is to simply reach out, but you may be looking for other ways you can be there for them.[1]

If you would like to send a gift, I want to share some we received that meant so much to us.

Before I do, a couple comments.

When sending gifts there's no need to send tracking information or check in to see if the gift was received. If you believe there may be an issue in receiving the gift, then send it with the signature required. You'll be able to know for sure that the gift was received, as well as get shipping updates along the way. While sending a gift is always meant with so much love, your loved one is already going through a hard time, and asking for extra details or confirmations will be hard at this time. These are the nuanced things that seem so tiny, but we don't often think about the receiver's perspective of what that experience will be like. The person grieving may barely want to get out of bed. They likely will not be actively checking tracking numbers. Any ounce of energy may be spent just trying to survive their day, so replying to a text asking for an update might feel like a big ask of them.

Here are gift ideas you can send along with any messages, cards, or emails.

DONATING TO AN ANIMAL SHELTER IN THEIR PET'S NAME

Here is an example we received. Our heart beat deep when we opened this card knowing Kingston had helped someone else.

Here is additional language if you want to send an email or text message to them:

> Hi [Name],
>
> I wanted to send you a note to let you know that we are thinking about you! We have donated to Donation Location in honor of your sweet [Pet name].
>
> We wanted to honor [his/her] life and pay forward some love to other for all the years of happiness [he/she] had and gave. I know that there wasn't a day in [his/her] life [he/she] didn't feel SO loved. How lucky [he/she] was to be part of the [Last name family].
>
> No need to reply but wanted to send some love.
>
> Sincerely,
>
> [your name]

Book *Signs*: The Secret Language of the Universe by Laura Lynne Jackson

Gift Message: The signs are real – I read a book about it after a friend who also lost a pup recommended it. It gave me so much peace. I thought it may give you peace.

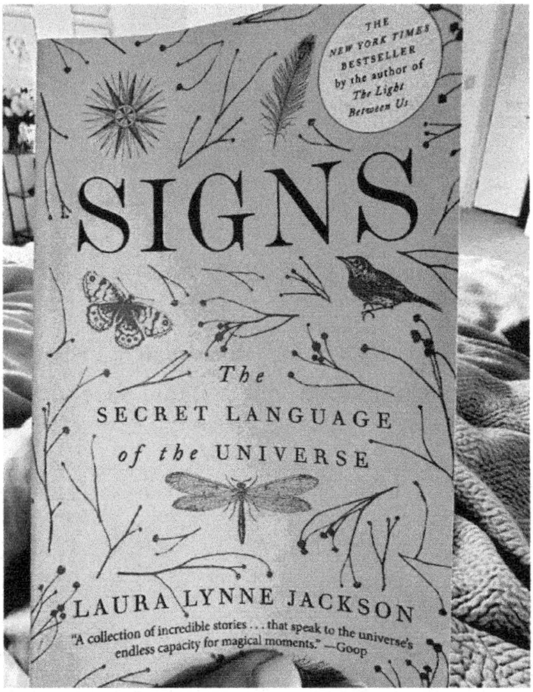

This book really did this for us. I referenced it often in my book and if you read it, you already know our sign, and how validating it is. It truly did and does bring peace.

Memorialight Modern Grief Gift 40 mm Crystal Ball Rainbow Maker Best for Daily Remembrance

This gift truly made me cry. I hung it immediately. Every day as the sun goes down the rays of rainbows dance around our room.

Paper Seeds

This gift was so special because our friend not only was able to find dog bone shaped ones, but also found Chinese Forget-Me-Nots. Our Kingston was a Chinese Shar Pei. Anytime you can connect something personal it elevates the gift even more.

PERSONALIZED PILLOW OR BLANKET

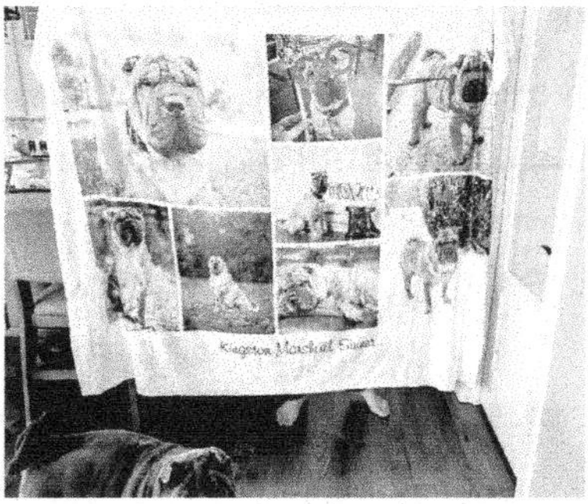

I will say to please think about the person you are sending these gifts to. I do believe they can be traumatizing to some. For me, in my first two weeks after losing Kingston I spent a lot of time crying in my closet alone wrapped up in these and hugging the pillow. They were therapy for me.

However, I now cannot have them out or displayed so I have them in a beautiful box that I can pull out when I need to grieve.

These can be purchased on any photo site like snapfish.com

A GARDEN STONE

This is truly special. It came beautifully packaged with a nice card. Purchased from Personalization Mall. Their website is www.personalizationmall.com. This was called Pet Memorial Heart Heard Stone.

It has Kingston's name on it. We placed it at our front door as Kingston was the protector of our home.

A TREE TO PLANT

We received a gift of a tree. We delayed planting it because, well, we are just not domesticated adults, ha! Eventually, we decided to work out some emotions by sweating in the Midwest heat and digging a hole in the ground to make room for our new tree. It continues to be a beautiful reminder of how we honor Kingston.

Truthfully, we may have cursed our friends, Amy and Kelly, a few times as we got started. The ground was hard and layered with rocks. We tried to figure out how to jump on the shovel to jam it into the ground (my idea that surprisingly worked!) The kids stood around us, clearly concerned and confused about what their parents were doing. We kept falling off, sweating more, adjusting strategies, taking turns, and finally… we did it. We got our tree planted for Kingston. We fell to the ground and burst into laughter. We felt silly in our approach and how much effort it took, but it felt good to accomplish something for our son. It was a genuine happiness we hadn't experienced in a while.

We planted our tree in Kingston's favorite back corner of our yard, it was a place that he went to everyday and looked back at his home. We hope our dogwood grows big and tall and that, one day, we place a bench in the shade.

PLANT A MEMORIAL TREE

This gift took me down an emotional path that I cannot explain. It was from my work team. Knowing 500 trees were planted in my Kingston's name still overwhelms my heart with a feeling of love I can hardly explain. I truly believe one tree would have made an impact, so you don't have to go for 500. This was a wonderful and special gift that I believe carries forward Kingston's legacy. It also meant a lot that they will be planted in the state Kingston was born.

Below is the gift message I received.

> Gift Message:
>
> In honor of Kingston, we wanted to give you something that would symbolize his enduring spirit and bring a sense of solace. We have arranged for a grove of 500 trees to be planted in his birth place of Texas. These trees will stand tall, providing shade and shelter to countless lives, just as Kingston provided comfort and joy to you.
>
> May this grove serve as a living tribute to the beautiful memories you shared and a reminder of the profound impact Kingston had on your life and the lives of everyone who knew him. And may it bring you peace in knowing that Kingston's legacy will flourish and contribute to the world's natural beauty for years to come.
>
> Love,
>
> Your Directorie Family www.thetreesremember.com

BEARAE DOG MEMORIAL GIFTS

Name of Gift when you google: Dog Candle Holder Statue, Pet Memorial Gifts, Pet Loss Gifts, Bereavement Gifts, Pet Sympathy Gifts for Loss of Dogs

An angel holding a pup is so comforting. I have two of these, but this one specifically I wanted to share because they found a wrinkly dog like my Kingston. The personalization of a gift can make it feel exponentially special.

Can be found on Amazon

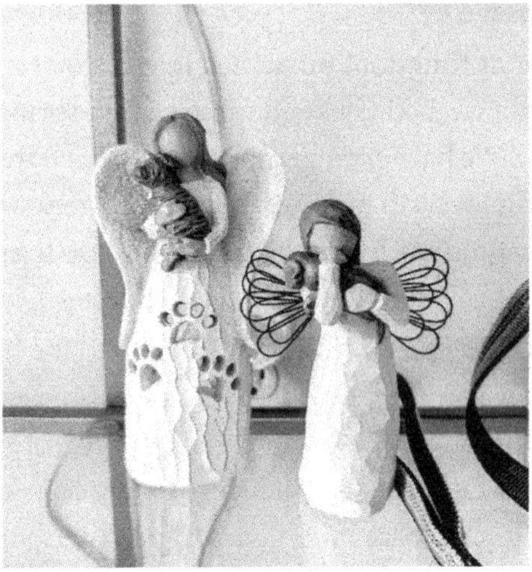

FLOWERS

Flowers arrived daily. It was magical. Our home smelled so fresh and each arrangement was so beautiful.

I really loved the message I received with these flowers. It was like she knew everything my heart was feeling:

Gift message: They won't really help, I know. They'll just bring in some color and something pretty when you're so low. I know. I know. I've cried for you and your Kingston many times over the last couple days. Do you want to cry to someone other than Chris? Feel free to call me. I can relate. Somehow, it's harder because they're so innocent and they don't know what's going on and you feel like you shouldn't have to decide and you know it's what's best. But it's just not the best too. I hate it for you so much.

Use whatever your heart tells you.

A HOLOGRAM OR "MEMORIAL LIGHT"

We received this and our hearts melted. We have it in a spot in our room that gives a little glow. I believe these can be purchased on amazon, or if you google, a lot will come up.

Gift message: "A light to shine in your home the way [pets name] continues to shine in your heart."

A REAL GOLD NECKLACE OR FINE PIECE OF JEWELRY

This gift really blew me away. It is in the shape of a crown for our boy's name, Kingston. I received this gift prior to Kington's passing and wore it with him. I haven't really taken it off since. I can work out and shower in it. It is from a beautiful jewelry store, and I imagine on the more expensive side, but I will cherish this forever. (thank you Kate!)

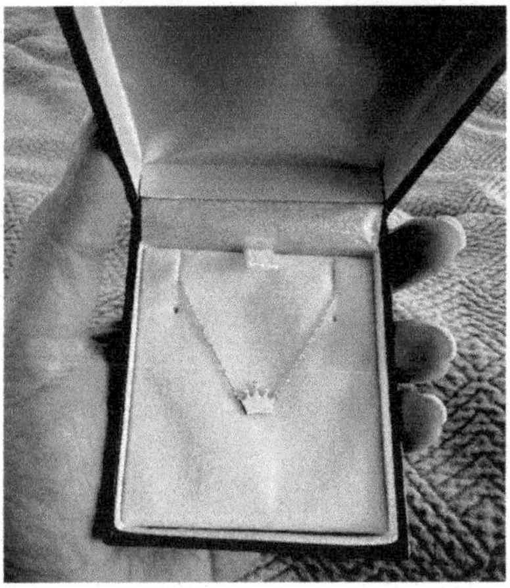

A BEAUTIFUL CARD WITH HAND DRAWN ART

This card came with a couple gifts, but I wanted to share the card alone as the little angel halo on one of the paws meant so much. My friend let me know her daughter drew it for us.

WINDCHIME

Gift message: "It broke my heart to see and feel your sadness. I wish there was something I could do to make the pain go away. Hoping this will help find a way to stay connected to him."

PICTURE FRAME

One approach can be inspirational or a special handcrafted frame. We loved the first one made by Mariposa. You can google: Mariposa SHINE BRIGHTLY LITTLE STAR Signature 4x6 Frame

The next frame was a gift I received right after Kingston passed. To be honest, I was not ready to receive this frame. The weight of the frame and the wording made it important, but I could feel there was a sentiment of "fun" that I was not ready to feel. My friend who gave this to me shared she purchased this frame the moment she got her first dog, Marvin, who has since passed. She said finding the perfect photo has made her smile each time she looks at it. She buys it for any friend who's pup passes.

I have to say, once I found the perfect photo of Kingston, I placed it in my closet where I see it every single day. And every single day it makes me smile.

I love this frame SO much. You can google this frame and wording under: Thanks For Everything I Had A Wonderful Time - In Memory Of Pet Picture Frame by House Parts

COMMISSION A WORK OF ART

A beautiful piece we have is from UglyCryClay artist Meagan Latch. You can find her precious work on Etsy or on Instagram.

It comes BEAUTIFULLY packaged, and it is hand crafted with so much love and care.

She has done incredible recreation of images. Some ideas include maybe just the pup alone, or in their favorite place, or if there is a family memory in the kitchen, or the pup watching over the house. Truly it's so beautiful.

COLLAGE PHOTO BEAUTIFULLY FRAMED

You can go through photos they have posted and create an album or enlarge and frame favorite pet pictures.

This can be found on www.snapfish.com

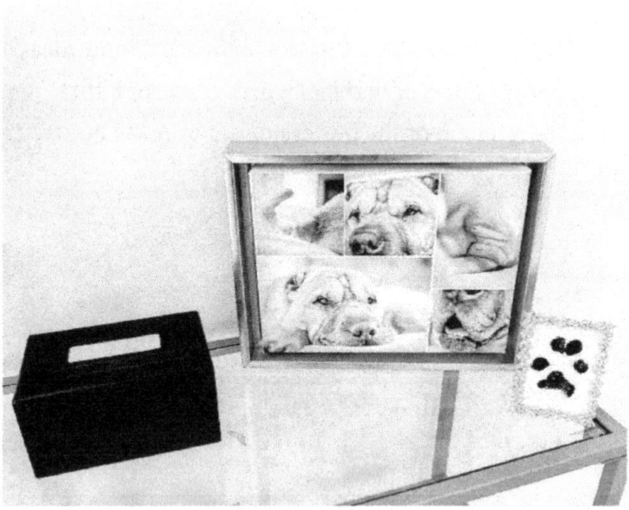

A TREAT

Our friends got creative and sent a Dairy Queen cake through Door Dash. The big thing here is it arrived at our door and we didn't have to go anywhere. It was also funny because they sent a note stating if we chose, we could eat our feelings away.

Another friend sent us a taco bar dinner from Costco this way with flowers. It truly was creative and made us smile.

BOX OF PHOTOS LIKE POLAROID IMAGES

I had been searching ways to soothe our hearts.

Creating this box and being intentional about finding moments to recall memories is an idea I had to share. I open the box and pull out a photo when I want to laugh or just to remember these special moments.

Loss and grief are such a force. I genuinely believe that they illustrate the sheer magnitude of the connection we shared and what love truly embodies. If you're also missing someone, consider making one of these for yourself or for someone. Instagram and socials are fun to go back and look at pictures, but stepping away from a screen, holding an actual memory, and talking about it has been such a gift.

The box can be found at a Home Goods, At Home store, or Amazon.

The photos can be done on www.snapfish.com by ordering their "Mini Photo Prints Set, Cardstock" option.

A FIGURINE

We received two types of figurines that looked like our pup. These are so precious. They both sit on the alter we created for Kingston.

The custom breed, color, and attention to detail really made these gifts so thoughtful and wonderful to receive.

All the gifts noted above are gifts we received and have cherished. We do not receive a commission or any type of sponsorship for including. They are just gifts we believe in. However, we cannot make any guarantees about the quality, reputation, ideologies, or business practices of the 3rd party companies that are included or how your loved one will respond.

Reference:

1. "6 Ways to Help a Friend Whose Pet Died." *Www.Thepetmemorial.Org.Com*, 2 Feb. 2021, thepetmemorial.org/six-ways-to-help-a-friend-whose-pet-died/. Accessed 11 Jun. 2023.

WORKPLACE SUPPORT: Creating a Supportive Environment

- Support for Organizational Pet Bereavement Inclusion. How to convince Human Resources
- FAQs and Email Template to meet with Human Resources
- Training for Leaders and Colleagues

Support for Organizational Pet Bereavement Inclusion. How to convince Human Resources

Changing the Paradigm

- 60% of private-sector workers get paid time off.1
- Grief-related losses cost U.S. companies as much as $75 billion annually.[1]

Yet the vast majority of employers provide only two to four days of bereavement leave, depending on whether the deceased is a child, spouse, parent or extended family member. On average, four days are allotted for the death of a spouse or child, according to the Society for Human Resource Management 2016 Paid Leave in the Workplace Survey. Three days are typically given for the loss of a parent, grandparent, domestic partner, sibling, grandchild or foster child. Only one or two days are usually offered for the death of a spouse's relative or an extended family member (aunt, uncle, cousin). And, for the death of a close friend or colleague, most companies don't extend any leave at all.[1]

- Grief experts recommend 20 days of bereavement leave for close family members. [1]
- 4 days is the average bereavement leave allotted for the death of a spouse or child. [1]
- 3 days is the average time off given for the loss of a parent, grandparent, domestic partner, sibling, grandchild or foster child. [1]

There is much to be done in how organizations can handle grief. This document is not to ask for additional time within your organizations bereavement policy, but instead to educate and inspire you to advocate for inclusion of Pets as part of your bereavement policy.

WHY LOSING A PET IS ESPECIALLY DIFFICULT[2]

It's common to think that people don't get that sad after loss of a pet. But research tells us that often, the grief that people feel following loss of an animal companion feels the same as grief following loss of a human companion. In some cases, people report even more intense feelings. This may be because of the special type of relationship we feel with our pets. Often, it feels like a parent-child relationship, and is associated with unconditional love and acceptance, which we don't always get in our human relationships. Feeling these especially strong feelings after pet loss may take some people by surprise and lead to feeling shame or guilt.

There are many reasons why grieving a pet can be just as or even more difficult than grieving a human:

- While everyone can understand and empathize with loss of a person, not everyone can grasp how devastating pet loss can be. Some people may make insensitive comments, such as "you can just get another pet," which adds to the sense that other people don't understand what we're going through.
- We don't tend to have the same rituals surrounding pet loss as we do with the loss of our fellow humans. This may include not getting as much social support from others. This may lead to feeling like our emotions aren't valid, and feeling even more isolated.
- Because some people don't understand pet loss, we often don't have as much space to process emotions. For example, pet loss is often not considered a valid reason for taking time off of work. People who have just lost a companion may find it extremely difficult to keep up with normal responsibilities, even though they are expected to keep performing as normal.
- Because of stigma surrounding grieving during pet loss, some people may find it hard to talk openly about what they are struggling with. Often, people who have lost a pet feel embarrassed or ashamed at the depth of their emotion.

Being hesitant to acknowledge or talk about these strong emotions is common. Not having solid support systems surrounding pet loss can sometimes make processing it more difficult. This may mean that the pet grieving process is more complex and it can take longer for us to move on.

Another difficulty surrounding pet loss that is often unacknowledged is that it leads to changes in a person's routine. Perhaps a person got used to being woken up in the morning by their hungry cat, or getting exercise through walking their dog. When that pet is gone, a person's whole daily routine may be thrown off, leaving a person feeling even more lost. Small hassles and disruptions to a person's routine can easily add up to be ***just as stressful and harmful to health*** than bigger events.

PET LOSS AND PHYSICAL HEALTH[2]

Grief from pet loss ***may also lead to physical symptoms***, such as fatigue, insomnia, a hollow feeling in the stomach, tightness in the chest, dry mouth, and aches and pains.

Sometimes, our reactions to grief can be severe. One woman ***reportedly*** experienced "broken heart syndrome" after losing her dog. This condition occurs when one chamber of the heart suddenly weakens in response to an emotional or physical stress. Its symptoms are similar to heart attack symptoms. While this condition is rare, it highlights the large effect that grief can have on the body.[2]

> "It was the most tragic, traumatic, and emotionally devastating experience I had ever been through. I didn't know what to do. I cried day and night." (Dorothy R., Alabama)[3]
>
> "I felt like someone had ripped out my insides." (Karen A., Illinois)[3]

Do these reactions to the loss of a pet touch a familiar chord in your heart? Grief, confusion, anger, guilt and depression are all typical responses to the death of a loved one. Only recently, however, have researchers come to realize that a pet may also be considered a loved one and a family member, and that its death may evoke similar and often equally intense emotions.[3]

There is an abundance of research on the physical and mental benefits of having a pet and/or utilizing an animal in therapy. However, the loss of that companion can be devastating and traumatic. Humans develop a lasting attachment with their pets, which breaks at the loss of the pet. Regardless of the manner of death, a pet owner may perceive the death as traumatic and experience distress or exhibit posttraumatic stress symptoms. Seeking psychotherapy for pet loss can help to alleviate the distress and process the complicated grief. Growth following a trauma allows individuals to find new understanding about themselves and the world. The loss of a beloved pet cannot be replaced, but rather humans can develop undiscovered meaning in light of a tragedy.[4]

Though discussion of the benefits of pet companionship is widely discussed, there is less information regarding pet loss, specifically traumatic pet loss. Traumatic grief is distinct in that the presentation of a person who experiences loss is met with significant separation distress as a result of the death of a loved one (Jacobs, Mazure, & Prigerson, 2000). The definition of trauma is not concrete and does not describe one type of event; trauma is subjective and is variably based on each individuals' experience to an event. A traumatic event, such as physical abuse or natural disaster, does not always result in someone developing posttraumatic stress disorder, instead, a person's emotional experience of the trauma determines the long-term effects (Center for Substance Abuse Treatment, 2014). [4]

Therefore, the loss of a pet can be interpreted by an individual as traumatic, similar to the loss of a family member, and breaking the human-animal bond.[4]

Here are some examples of how other companies are managing:

Mastercard's policy is a direct result of CEO Ajay Banga speaking with Sandberg about her book, Fraccaro says. "Although bereavement leave is not one of the things you automatically think about when you are deciding whether to join a company, it is one aspect of the employee value proposition," he says.[1]

Facebook and Mastercard have set a high standard, and many smaller companies may not be in a position to dole out a month's worth of paid leave—for any reason. Fortunately, there are creative ways HR professionals can support employees when they need it most. For instance, if a worker needs more time off following the death of a loved one, consider asking other staff members to donate vacation time.[1]

That's the approach used by Joyce Van Curen, HR director at Turning Point Community Programs, a nonprofit mental health agency in Sacramento, Calif., with 620 employees. Typically, donations pour in and the grieving individual winds up with more leave than he or she needs, Van Curen says. If the grief is profound, Van Curen will encourage the employee to get a note from his or her doctor saying additional time off is needed, so that she can put the employee on family medical leave.[1]

> **'Grievers have told me that what was most disruptive to them is they felt they needed to go back to work soon and they got judged on that.'** [1]
>
> —*David Kessler, Grief.com*

It's essential that co-workers, HR and managers acknowledge that a huge loss has occurred in the employee's life, Kessler says. He offers these guidelines for dealing with an employee who has lost a loved one[1]:

- Ask the employee, or a co-worker who is close to the worker, how he or she would like you to communicate with staff that he or she will be out of the office. If the bereaved individual doesn't want to share much, simply state, "Jane had a loss in her immediate family and will be out for the next week."
- Be aware of when the funeral is taking place and whether the employee is traveling to get there. Refrain from contacting the employee during those times, and ask the person's manager to do the same.
- Avoid telling the employee you know what he or she is going through. Nobody knows what it's like to have a spouse, child

or parent die suddenly unless they have been through it themselves—and even then the experience is highly personal and individual. That said, if you haven't yet experienced the death of a close family member and want to get a better understanding of what it feels like, ask trusted colleagues who have been through it if they're willing to share their story so you can better relate to other employees.

- Send flowers and, if the funeral is local, request that one or two representatives from the office attend. If possible, make a donation in the loved one's memory to a recommended charity. At the very least, have everyone sign a card.

If the employee learns about the death while at work, he or she will often come to HR with the news—so remember to expect the unexpected. Van Curen suggests keeping a binder of resources on hand. "You can't give advice," she says, "but you can provide resources for grief counselors, funeral homes, tax attorneys and florists."[1]

Changing the Paradigm[1]

Most people feel isolated after a family member dies, even if they are from a large family, Mason says. Often, others want to help but don't know what to do, so they do nothing—which makes the bereaved person feel even more alone, she says. Offer to mow the lawn, pick up food at the grocery store, walk the dog or plan an outing for their children. [1]

"I couldn't understand when friends didn't ask me how I was," writes Sandberg in *Option B*. "I felt invisible, as if I was standing in front of them but they couldn't see me." [1]

Keep in mind that the first year is typically the toughest, as individuals navigate all the milestones, anniversaries and birthdays without their loved one for the first time, Mason says. [1]

The more flexible an employer can be during this most difficult time, the more loyalty it will get in return over the long run. "If the employee has been with you a year or longer, and they're a good employee," Van Curen says, "why would you throw that away and not do everything in your power to support that person?" [1]

Pets can actually **make us healthier people**. Those who have pets tend to have lower rates of heart disease and lower blood pressure. Some studies have found that they are also less likely to experience loneliness or depression, and more likely to say they are satisfied with their life. So it may be no surprise that when we lose this relationship, our health is affected in a negative way.[2]

Again, the goal of receiving this document is not to expand additional days to your bereavement policy, but instead to educate and inspire you to advocate for inclusion of pet loss as part of your bereavement policy.

References:

1. Roepe, L. R. (2023, January 20). How to Support Employees through Grief and Loss. *SHRM*. https://www.shrm.org/hr-today/news/hr-magazine/0917/pages/how-to-support-employees-through-grief-and-loss.aspx
2. Connor, B., MD. (2021b, February 26). *Grieving the Loss of a Pet - Brynna Connor MD*. Brynna Connor MD. https://doctorconnor.com/grieving-the-loss-of-a-pet/#:~:text=Pet%20Loss%20and%20Mental%20Health&text=Some%20people%20experience%20mental%20symptoms,and%20depression%20for%20some%20people.
3. *The Emotions of Pet Loss*. (n.d.-b). The Pet Loss Support Page. https://www.pet-loss.net/emotions.shtml
4. *Traumatic Pet Loss | Society for the Advancement of Psychotherapy*. (n.d.). https://societyforpsychotherapy.org/traumatic-pet-loss/

FAQs and Email Template to meet with Human Resources

FAQ's for your HR Team

If you would like to champion to have pets added to your organization's bereavement policies, we want you to be prepared. Being prepared is not only having the facts, but also being ready to answer questions your Human Resources Department may have as well as the executive team. It's often not just about convincing your HR team, but also helping HR to make this pitch to other executives to get approved. We want to arm you and them with talking points to help navigate questions that executives may have.

How many days of bereavement leave do you propose for pets?

- Grieving looks different for everyone, so as much as the company can support.
- Even just 1 day would be appreciated and a great first step to supporting more employees.

What do we do with employees that have multiple pets?

- In order to fully support employees during these difficult times we should extend this for all pets, as the bond is no different between a dog or a bird.
- A letter or email from an established veterinary practice could help support an employee's claims of a pet or help mitigate potential abuse of the policy.

Are companies legally obligated to offer this leave?

- While it is not a legal obligation, it is an ethical one to support all members of our people community.

How do we ask for proof (since there likely will not be a published obituary)?

- A letter or email from an established veterinary practice.

How will implementing compassionate leave for pets help the bottom line?

- We know that turnover across companies is at an all time high in many industries. Supporting employees and showing appreciation for their lives outside of work has been proven to help reduce turnover and increase employee retention.
- When an employee loses a pet, even if bereavement leave is not offered, chances are that the employee is not going to be productive during this difficult time. By offering them space to heal and rest they can come back and be more focused and productive.
- Offering more compassionate policies in the workplace is excellent PR for recruiting top talent. Who doesn't want to work somewhere that cares about employees as people?

Below is a potential email to Human Resources that you can attach to the Changing the Paradigm PDF. This could also be included in an invite to meet if you want to set up time to discuss.

> Dear [HR Professional],
>
> There is an employee benefit that I think would provide great value to [insert organization name]. Many of our teammates have special family members that are currently overlooked by our leave policy and that is our beloved pets.
>
> Attached you will find some information on the importance and benefits of providing leave to care for and bereavement time for our pet family members. I know that supporting our teammates is important to you and it's important to me as well. It would mean a lot to me for you to consider updating our company's policy.
>
> I understand that any change in benefits may need to be considered by multiple people. Please let me know how I can support you in this effort. If you would like to speak

> more about this, I would welcome the opportunity for us to meet or have a call.

This document was made in partnership with Erin Barr Consulting. Erin specializes in providing businesses with customized Human Resources solutions to fit their needs. Offering flexible and comprehensive offerings to help organizations meet and exceed their goals. For more information, please visit https://www.erinabarr.com. Knowledgeable HR help is just a phone call away.

Training for Leaders and Colleagues

Manager and Team Training

PET LOSS AND PHYSICAL HEALTH[1]

Grief from pet loss may also lead to physical symptoms, such as fatigue, insomnia, a hollow feeling in the stomach, tightness in the chest, dry mouth, and aches and pains.

Sometimes, our reactions to grief can be severe. One woman reportedly experienced "broken heart syndrome" after losing her dog. This condition occurs when one chamber of the heart suddenly weakens in response to an emotional or physical stress. Its symptoms are similar to heart attack symptoms. While this condition is rare, it highlights the large effect that grief can have on the body.

WHY LOSING A PET IS ESPECIALLY DIFFICULT[1]

It's common to think that people don't get that sad after loss of a pet. But research tells us that often, the grief that people feel following loss of an animal companion feels the same as grief following loss of a human companion. In some cases, people report even more intense feelings. This may be because of the special type of relationship we feel with our pets. Often, it feels like a parent-child relationship, and is associated with unconditional love and acceptance, which we don't always get in our human relationships. Feeling these especially strong feelings after pet loss may take some people by surprise and lead to feeling shame or guilt.

There are ***many reasons*** why grieving a pet can be just as or even more difficult than grieving a human:

- While everyone can understand and empathize with loss of a person, not everyone can grasp how devastating pet loss can be. Some people may make insensitive comments, such as "you can just get another pet," which adds to the sense that other people don't understand what we're going through.

- We don't tend to have the same rituals surrounding pet loss as we do with the loss of our fellow humans. This may include not getting as much social support from others. This may lead to feeling like our emotions aren't valid, and feeling even more isolated.
- Because some people don't understand pet loss, we often don't have as much space to process emotions. For example, pet loss is often not considered a valid reason for taking time off of work. People who have just lost a companion may find it extremely difficult to keep up with normal responsibilities, even though they are expected to keep performing as normal.
- Because of stigma surrounding grieving during pet loss, some people may find it hard to talk openly about what they are struggling with. Often, people who have lost a pet feel embarrassed or ashamed at the depth of their emotion.

Being hesitant to acknowledge or talk about these strong emotions is common. Not having solid support systems surrounding pet loss can sometimes make processing it more difficult. This may mean that the pet grieving process is more complex and it can take longer for us to move on.

Another difficulty surrounding pet loss that is often unacknowledged is that it leads to changes in a person's routine. Perhaps a person got used to being woken up in the morning by their hungry cat, or getting exercise through walking their dog. When that pet is gone, a person's whole daily routine may be thrown off, leaving a person feeling even more lost. Small hassles and disruptions to a person's routine can easily add up to be just as stressful and harmful to health than bigger events.[1]

> *"It was the most tragic, traumatic, and emotionally devastating experience I had ever been through. I didn't know what to do. I cried day and night." (Dorothy R., Alabama)*[2]

> *"I never knew anything could hurt so bad. I cried a whole ocean of tears. I went through self-hatred for putting my pet to sleep, to depression, to acceptance. For a long time I couldn't even watch a dog food commercial." (Cheryl T., Alabama)*[2]

Do these reactions to the loss of a pet touch a familiar chord in your heart? Grief, confusion, anger, guilt and depression are all typical responses to the death of a loved one. Only recently, however, have researchers come to realize that a pet may also be considered a loved one and a family member, and that its death may evoke similar and often equally intense emotions.[2]

Real Life Example handled with an employee related to their brother. The same principles apply for pets.[3]

Sam walked up, teary-eyed and with a look of distress across his face. My mind flashed to every possibility. I knew it wasn't good… but I had no idea what it could be.

As we sat down with one another, alone in the conference room, he looked down, took a deep breath, and in a shaking voice said, *"I just found out my brother died."*

Would you know what to say if that happened to one of your team members?[3]

It's the last thing in the world you want to happen to anyone, but the reality is that sometimes tragedy falls on those closest to us. And when it's one of your own employees, it's important to know how to respond and support them.

Your first response is one of the most important moments after finding out about a team member's loss. You might not know exactly what to say, but if you know how to respond well, it will speak volumes and mean a lot to the impacted team member.

How to Respond When You First Find Out[3]

Author and speaker Mark Crowley says the best thing you can do after learning that a team member has lost a loved one is to **call and offer your support.**

> *"It's tempting to believe employees don't want to be "bothered" by their boss in their time of grief and mourning... But* ***in moments of deep loss, human beings need to feel supported and cared for*** *by the people closest to them."*

If you're a leader that cares, or as Mark likes to say, **Leads from the Heart**, your words will matter quite a bit to your team member. You may even be the first person in the company they tell.

> *"Telling someone directly that* ***you are profoundly sorry for their loss, and that you empathize with all the pain*** *they are feeling goes right to their hearts."*

This kind of thoughtfulness makes a big impact and shows your team member know that you're there for them.

Tell them about your company's bereavement policy[3]

After that initial call or meeting, if you haven't already, check what your company's bereavement policy is and any local laws. This takes the burden off of them figuring it out, so they know how many days they're allowed to take off, as well as other important details.

According to the US Department of Labor, there is no national law requiring any paid leave, but there is *unpaid* time off permitted under the Family Medical Leave Act and to attend funerals. This means their options will really vary state to state and company to company.

Once you know what your company's policy officially is, let your team member know you found the information while you were looking into ways you could help. Best of all, this can potentially get HR or another leader involved to help and show support as well. Especially at smaller companies, you can expect others will want to help and express condolences, too.

Regardless of how much time they take, realize you will need to give them time to get back on their feet. While no amount of time can completely heal the pain caused by a tragic loss, time off and lightening their burden of work can make a big difference.

What to do while they've gone on bereavement[3]

While your grieving team member is away, it's important to have a game plan, especially if it could be an extended leave. The smaller your team, the less you can afford to be without a single team member, so it's important to know how to balance being empathetic with making sure the work gets done.

Crowley says he's often seen selfish managers respond to an employee's loss from the perspective of what they're losing– seeing their goals and deadlines slip through their fingers due to the loss of a team member. These managers may say tone-deaf things like:

> *I know you've suffered a great loss, but do you have any sense on when you might be back at work?*

Crowley understands how this can happen, but does not excuse it:

> *"You might gasp at this, but workplace pressures seem so great at times that many of us lose sight of what behavior is most appropriate, and* ***we end up thinking more about ourselves than our employee."***

The reality is, all of us will be impacted by the loss of a loved one at different points in our lives. It's important to be as empathetic as possible while thinking about the best way to move forward.

So what do you do? Here's what Crowley recommends[3]:

> *"When a member of your team suffers a great loss,* ***the leader's job is to circle the wagons****, bring the team together and divvy up the employee's workload until they return. Even in times of great loss, most people tend to feel guilty about being away. So* ***what they need in the moment is to***

> ***hear their boss say, 'Please don't worry about work. We've got you covered.'"***

Crowley says that managers often fail to recognize how critical a moment it is for their reputation as a leader:

> *"It's in these critical moments when* ***people decide if you're a boss worth striving for– or even working for."*** *Make sure your response says, "We're here for you."*

Plan for while they're gone, *and* their return[3]

Being empathetic is important, but it's equally important to not overlook the importance of having a game plan for how you're going to cover the team member's workload while they're gone.

Crowley shared with us a story of a previous manager of his whose five-year-old died suddenly. When she took a two-month leave, her team stepped up and took on the job of managing themselves.

However, over time, he could see that the pressure was taking a toll. Without a proper manager to lead the team, the absence caused a block that affected the team making matters worse, when she returned, there were new problems and challenges.

> *"It quickly became clear she was not sufficiently healed. She would come to work, but close her door. Or she would leave after only a few hours,"*

Ultimately, after much patience, things didn't work out. Crowley says that if it happened again, he'd still offer the person the same compassion and support as before. However, he'd have had a better plan for her and the team:

> *"I will always regret not realizing that I had a business to run...and that when she went out on extended bereavement leave, I could have found a new manager to lead her team."*

By finding a replacement to fill the space the grieving manager left, it would have been a win-win: the manager would be given the time they need while the pressure on your end for them to come back is removed.

Then, when they do return, he could have found a role that better fit what she was ready for, without the pressure of her full team right off the bat.

Speaker & consultant, Mark C. Crowley is the author of Lead From The Heart, Transformational Leadership For The 21st Century. Connect with him via his website at www.markccrowley.com.

What to do when they get back[3]

Now that your team member is back in the office, it's important not to make assumptions, whether that's assuming everything is back to normal or that they want to take it slow.

Everyone deals with grief differently, and often the most difficult part about coming back to work isn't the work itself, but the response from their boss and co-workers.

You need to feel out how they're doing and see how they want to move forward. If you're not sure if they're up for moving forward with their 1-on-1s right now, **ask them.**

- **Did they say yes?** They probably want to get back to work. Work allows us to keep busy and connect with others, both of which can help someone experiencing grief. Find out what they need to feel like they can catch up and feel productive. Prioritize, remove blockers, and lend a hand where you can.
- **Did they say no, hesitate, or pause?** Let them set the pace and give them time to get back into the office flow. If you're already meeting with them and you get the feeling they're not comfortable opening up, throw out the agenda and let them talk about whatever they feel like.

This is where having an emotional savings account built up can really help. If they already trust you, they will know you have their best interests at heart, and will be more willing to open up about how they're feeling.

How to handle bereavement with a new team member[3]

What if the employee who experienced the loss is new to the team?

Without any previous connection established, it can make the situation even more difficult to handle.

What can you do? [3]

Leadership coach and **Executive Velocity** founder Beth Miller coached an executive in exactly this position.

The executive did everything she could think of: attend the funeral, expressed her condolences, and even offered a donation in honor of the employee's loved one. Those were immediate and thoughtful things she could do.

Unfortunately, it was after this that the difficult part began. As Miller recalls:

> *"When the employee returned to work, she expressed her sorrow for his loss. She then followed with the question: "is there anyone that you can talk to about your loss?"*
> *This question demonstrated her concern but didn't commit her to be a grief counselor, and the answer provided her with the name of the person he felt close to in the organization. She also reminded him of the company's EAP, employee assistance program.*

By taking the issue head on from the start, the executive made sure that the employee got the help and support they needed. Then, over time, she kept an eye on how they were doing on their journey of moving forward.

> *"She then became keenly aware of the employee's behaviors,* ***looking for early warning signs*** *that could impact his productivity such as sick days or disengagement.*
> *In this case, the employee's energy and interaction with other team members did not seem to change.*

> *She also checked in with the employee's close friend, to learn if she was missing anything about the employee's recovery from loss.*
>
> *During the next few months she sporadically checked in with both him and his close colleague to see how he was doing and if he needed any additional assistance. She believed that having another employee to check in on the grieving employee was critical to success.*

And this effort she took to support her grieving employee made a real difference. According to Miller, two years later, the employee is still with the company and has taken on more responsibilities.

Speaker and leadership authority Beth Miller is the Leadership Executive Advisor and founder of Executive Velocity and Chair with Vistage. Learn more about her work at executive-velocity.com/.

What Do You Say to an Employee who has Suffered a Loss? [3]

One of the most difficult things about this type of situation, before even your response as their manager, is just how to be an **empathetic human being** to someone who has experienced loss.

What do you say to someone who has just had one of the most important people in their life taken from them?

For those who haven't experienced a similar loss, our first response– while meaning well– can be more harmful than anything without us even knowing it.

> *"I have learned that I never really knew what to say to others in need,"* Sandberg says. *"I tried to assure people that it would be okay, thinking that hope was the most comforting thing I could offer."*

Dailey echoed this, expressing that to someone experiencing grief, **words of hope show a lack of empathy** for what the person is going through:

> *"You carry that weight for the rest of your life. You do not shed it by getting over it. It changes you and becomes a part of you."*

The last thing you want is to say the wrong thing, so be careful falling on cliches or saying something that doesn't help them.

What to avoid saying[3]

A friend of Sandberg's with late-stage cancer once told her that **the worst thing someone could say to him was,** *"It's going to be okay."*

However, it wasn't until her own experience that she realized what he had meant.

> *"Real empathy is sometimes not insisting that it will be okay but acknowledging that it is not."*

Those who have experienced loss know that it's a pain that will never fully go away. Unfortunately, it's something that's difficult for those who haven't experienced something similar to understand, which is a big reason for this post.

Sandberg says even a well-intentioned, *"How are you?"* can trigger strong feelings:

> *"When I am asked 'How are you?' I stop myself from shouting, 'My husband died a month ago, how do you think I am?'"*

Similarly, anything that presumes the loss will go away– or tries to make it so– should be stayed away from, including:

- *"You're going to be fine."*
- *"Time is the great healer."*
- *"They're in a better place."*

What if you just found out about a team member's loss– or they just got back in the office– and you want to show your support? What do you say instead?

What to say instead[3]

Instead of, "*How are you,*" Sandberg says "*How are you today*" is better:

> *"When I hear, 'How are you today?' I realize the person knows that* ***the best I can do right now is to get through each day."***

Alternatively, Dailey says,

> *"It's odd but* ***I've felt the most comforted*** *when team members and friends say,* ***'I'm sorry. I don't know what to say.'"***

Here are a few more ideas of things you can say to express your support to a grieving employee:

- *"We're here for you." (Show empathy without trying to change how they're feeling.)*
- *"What can we do to help you right now?" (Like Sheryl's suggestion, you focus on immediate needs)*
- *"I'd love to talk if you're up for it. It's ok either way." (Extend the offer without making them feel like they have to respond or commit to anything.)*

Support Your Team When They Need it Most[3]

Having a team member go through bereavement at work is a situation no manager wants to experience.

Unfortunately, it's a part of life – and knowing how to handle it can make the recovery process easier for both them and the rest of your team.

Thanks to Mark Crowley and Beth Miller for their insights. And a special thanks to Travis Dailey for being kind enough to open up about his experience so that others who have experienced loss may benefit (and so that we can support them better).

You can read more from Travis at his personal site: travisdailey.com.

Getting out of bed is a herculean task. Meals no longer seem important. And work? That's just impossible. Understanding this is important because it is how your employee is feeling.

When To Ask An Employee To Return To Work[4]

Asking an employee about their return to work after the death of a loved one can be a tricky situation. If your organization already has a well-established bereavement policy, you may be able to look at those guidelines before the employee takes the leave.

With that policy, the framework and expectations are set at the beginning and there is no confusion over the process. You will also need to make sure this policy is included in your employee handbook so that everyone has access to it.

Still, flexibility in this bereavement period is important. The grieving employee may need more time than initially considered and they may not be able to communicate as well as you have come to expect from them.

During the bereavement leave, keep communication brief. Make initial contact after the death, offer condolences, and set into motion any planning for bereavement leave. During this contact, plan a second date and time for contact around the employee's schedule but do not push for too many details or plans.

During this second planned contact time, you can begin to ask about their anticipated return to work. Granted, you should use your best judgment on when and how to begin this conversation, as you will want to treat the subject with care. Don't rush them into giving you a date if they do not offer one. Instead, let them lead the conversation initially and see if they have a plan for their return.

If they don't seem to have a set date or time for their return, you may want to ask some gentle questions to nudge the conversation in that direction.

> Questions like *"Do you need to have someone cover your next shift?"* or *"Should we contact [another employee] and give them notes for next week's project?"* may steer the conversation in that direction.

If that doesn't work, it may be time to ask the question directly. Make sure you do so in a gentle manner and give them some time to reply.

You might have to discuss the limits of the bereavement policy, though be prepared for them to ask for additional time off if it seems they are still struggling with grief.

How To Support Employees Through Grief & Loss[4]

When someone dies, that death sends ripples outward among everyone and everything in their lives. It's no surprise this affects their professional lives as well. If you have an employee suffering from such a loss, it can create an often sudden and complicated situation for your organization.

With that in mind, we've created a guide for employers who may be seeking assistance in managing and supporting their employees when the worst happens and offers ideas for when an employee needs time off and how to assist when your employee returns to work. After all, an ounce of prevention is worth a pound of cure.

Support immediately after loss[4]

When tragedy strikes and loss occurs, the impact it has on a person can be tremendous. Employers can assist their employees in the immediate aftermath of loss by giving them the time that they need with their families and to grieve their loss without the added pressure of work responsibilities.

Depending on their individual policies and procedures, employers have a couple of different options. These are the two most common types of leave offered to employees after suffering the loss of an immediate family member.

Company Bereavement Policy

Bereavement leave is time off an employee can take after the death of a close family member or loved one. From an HR perspective, it is designed to give an employee some time off work to focus on their physical and mental wellbeing in the aftermath of a loss. In most cases, this includes a set amount of paid time following a death in an employee's family.

Bereavement policies are not required by law (except in the state of Oregon), but some states and cities have begun creating legislation that may eventually enact them. However, most companies offer some form of bereavement policy as part of their employee benefits.

If your company does not offer an official bereavement policy, you should consider one. Having a structured policy that addresses an employee's needs offers stability, certainty, and guarantees equity to those who require time off during a difficult time.

It also benefits the company as it grants an employee time to mourn without the pressures of their job and allows them to return to work with better clarity and productivity.

Employee Leave Donation

Some companies create Leave Donation or Leave Sharing programs. These programs allow employees to donate their accrued paid time off (PTO), vacation, or sick leave to other employees who may need emergency time off in the form of medical or family emergencies. Typically, this donated leave time goes into a pool to be used as needed.

Programs like this have been shown to increase employee morale, productivity, and even improve employee retention! If you do not have such a program but are curious about how they work and how to implement them, there are many online guides that provide more details on the topic.

SUPPORT UPON RETURN TO WORK[4]

When your employee does return to work after the death of a loved one, you may struggle with knowing how to support them while still maintaining a productive work environment for the entire company. Here are some tips on how to make this transition as painless as possible for everyone.

Be Patient And Give Them Space

The best way you can show that the employee that you care is to be patient and allow them the time to make any arrangements related to their loved ones passing. This can also include understanding their need for additional assistance (such as a grief counselor or outside help).

Show your concern at the outset but do not overwhelm them with work concerns or even your own condolences. When it comes to their work productivity, you especially need to be patient with any bumps or difficulties along the way. They may need a little longer to get back into their routine.

Offer Resources

One of the best things you can do is to make sure your employee knows what resources are available to them. Can you offer flexible scheduling for a few weeks? Perhaps there are options to work from home until they are able to come back into the office regularly.

You can encourage them to speak to HR or to any counselors your company has on retainer for just such times. Make sure they know what benefits they are entitled to and how to access them.

Delegate Responsibilities

Anyone coming back to work after an extended period of time off is likely going to need a little time to adjust. For someone coming back after bereavement leave, it can be even more difficult to catch up on everything they missed. They're also likely not at their most productive. This may be a good time to delegate some responsibilities to other coworkers until they feel confident enough to handle their previous workload.

Choose A Gift To Express Sympathy & Care

As coworkers, we often want to show that we support and care but aren't really sure what to do. Group or individual grieving gifts such as flowers and a card are wonderful ways to show a coworker that you are sorry for their loss.

And depending on the nature of your relationship, don't be afraid to think outside the box. Personalized memorial gifts such as photo engraved jewelry, memorial bookmarks and memorial coins can be personalized with a memory of their loved one.

Not only are these gifts highly personal but they also provide family, friends and even coworkers with a unique opportunity to show them how much they are cared for and supported during this time of grief.

Respect Their Privacy

Your employee doesn't owe you the intimate details of their situation. Nor should you pressure them into giving more information that is strictly necessary to make arrangements for their leave. This extends to sharing any details you do know with their coworkers or other people in the company. Your employee has a right to privacy and, as their boss, you owe them that level of respect.

References:

1. Connor, B., MD. (2021, February 26). *Grieving the Loss of a Pet - Brynna Connor MD.* Brynna Connor MD. https://doctorconnor.com/grieving-the-loss-of-a-pet/#:~:text=Pet%20Loss%20and%20Mental%20Health&text=Some%20people%20experience%20mental%20symptoms,and%20depression%20for%20some%20people.
2. *The Emotions of Pet Loss.* (n.d.). The Pet Loss Support Page. https://www.pet-loss.net/emotions.shtml
3. Evanish, J. (2022). Bereavement at Work: How to Help Employees During Tragedy. *Lighthouse - Blog About Leadership & Management Advice.* https://getlighthouse.com/blog/bereavement-at-work/
4. Evrmemories.com. (n.d.). *Going Back To Work After A Death In The Family.* https://www.evrmemories.com/going-back-to-work-after-a-death

VETERINARY PRACTICE SUPPORT:
Nurturing Compassionate Care

- Improving Protocols for Pet Euthanasia Support at Veterinary Offices
- Training Veterinary Staff in Compassionate Phone Communication and Pre-planning for Pet Euthanasia
- Doctor's Discussion Guide: Euthanasia Decision for Your Client's Beloved Pet

Improving Protocols for Pet Euthanasia Support at Veterinary Offices

Empathy Training for Veterinarians and Technicians

Compassion and empathy training for veterinarians and technicians should be a core component of their professional development. Training could be focus on active listening and validating emotions, allowing clients to express their feelings openly without fear of judgment. Professionals should be encouraged to use phrases like "I'm here for you," "I'm so sorry for your loss," and "Take all the time you need" to convey understanding and support during this difficult time.

Creating a Compassionate Reception Area

A fundamental step in protocols for pet euthanasia support is preparing the reception area.

Being aware of the types of appointments scheduled that day could make a world of difference. For those coming in for euthanasia replacing casual greetings with compassionate acknowledgments can make a significant difference. For instance, asking, "Is there anything specific we can do to make this process more comfortable for you and your pet?" can show genuine care and support.

By knowing the types of appointments scheduled that day will also allow employees greeting clients coming in with proper care and not assuming they are coming in for boarding or grooming.

Conclusion:

The stories shared by individuals like Molly, and countless others who have experienced pet loss, have emphasized simple and free protocol enhancements that only require a little bit of effort. By providing empathy training and creating compassionate reception areas we can ensure that pet owners are met with the understanding, support, and respect they deserve during these emotionally challenging moments. Normalizing discussions around pet grief is not only vital for healing but also essential for acknowledging the significant role our beloved pets play in our lives and the profound impact of their loss.

Training Veterinary Staff in Compassionate Phone Communication and Pre-planning for Pet Euthanasia

Compassionate Phone Communication

Effective and compassionate phone communication is crucial when discussing pet euthanasia with pet owners. Staff should be trained to approach these conversations with utmost sensitivity and empathy as well as what the office process is so they can communicate and set proper expectations.

Beginning the conversation with a warm greeting and acknowledging the emotional nature of the discussion can immediately set a supportive tone. Encourage staff to actively listen to the pet parent's feelings and concerns, without interrupting or rushing. Empathetic responses such as "I understand how difficult this decision is for you" or "I'm here to guide you through this process with care" can provide much-needed reassurance. Remember to use clear and gentle language to explain the euthanasia process, avoiding jargon or technical terms that might cause confusion or anxiety. It may be helpful to consider providing a phone script.

Pre-planning and Decision-Making

To alleviate stress during the difficult time of euthanasia, encourage staff to offer pre-planning options. When scheduling the appointment, gently inquire if the pet parent wishes to keep the leash, have a paw print, or select an urn and recording their preferences. By addressing these decisions ahead of time, it allows pet owners to make thoughtful choices without feeling rushed or overwhelmed during the euthanasia procedure.

Invoice Delivery with Sensitivity

Sending invoices for euthanasia services requires special consideration to be sensitive to the emotional state of the pet owner. Instead of sending the invoice in the middle of the workday, which can be jarring and unexpected, advise staff to schedule it for a time when the pet parent is more likely to be emotionally prepared. Consider sending the invoice later in the evening or on weekends. Moreover, it's essential to accompany the invoice with a heartfelt message expressing condolences and support. This small gesture can show compassion and understanding, reaffirming that the veterinary practice is there to support them during their time of grief.

Conclusion:

Compassionate phone communication plays a significant role in guiding pet owners through the difficult process of pet euthanasia. By offering pre-planning options and thoughtfully considering various steps in the process like the timing of invoice delivery, veterinary staff can support pet parents with empathy and care during these emotionally challenging times. Prioritizing sensitivity and understanding ensures that pet owners feel heard, supported, and guided through the process of saying goodbye to their beloved companions.

Doctor's Discussion Guide: Euthanasia Decision for Your Client's Beloved Pet

The following is a discussion guide veterinarians may consider using when discussing euthanasia with pet parents.

Introduction:

As veterinarians, we understand that the decision to euthanize a beloved pet is one of the most challenging and emotional moments for any pet parent. Our priority is to support you during this difficult time with compassion and understanding. We want you to feel empowered to ask questions, understand our process, and ensure that this time is entirely about you and your precious companion.

Let Them Know It's Okay To Express Feelings and Concerns

When discussing euthanasia, please don't hesitate to share your feelings and concerns with us. We genuinely care about you and your pet, and we want to provide the best possible support. Feel free to express any fears, doubts, or emotions you may be experiencing. We are here to listen without judgment and to offer guidance based on our experience and expertise.

Understand the Euthanasia Process

Our primary goal is to ensure a peaceful and painless process for your pet. We will walk you through the entire euthanasia procedure, explaining each step with clarity and compassion. This may include the method of euthanasia, the use of sedatives to ensure your pet's comfort, and the option to be present during the process if you wish. We encourage you to be present with your pet and be a part of sending them on their journey. It has been our experience pet parents who have chosen not to be there have regretted the decision. We also encourage you to ask any questions or seek clarification on any aspect of the procedure to put your mind at ease.

Pre-planning and Aftercare Decisions

Pre-planning can make the process more manageable for you and your pet. We'll discuss options such as keeping the leash, having a paw print, or selecting an urn for your pet's ashes. Making these decisions ahead of time can help alleviate any additional stress on the day of the euthanasia. Moreover, we will explain our aftercare options, including individual or communal cremation, as well as the return of your pet's ashes.

Your Needs Come First

During this time, it's essential to remember that you are not bothering us. Your pet's well-being and your emotional needs are our top priority. We are here to support you through every step of the process and to provide a safe space for you to grieve. Feel free to reach out to us with any questions, concerns, or requests you may have. Your grief is valid, and we are here to provide a listening ear and a compassionate heart.

Conclusion:

The decision to euthanize a beloved pet is incredibly difficult, and we understand the pain you may be experiencing. Please know that we are here for you, and our goal is to ensure that your pet's passing is peaceful and filled with love. You are not alone in this journey, and we encourage you to lean on us for support during this challenging time. Our practice is dedicated to providing the utmost care and understanding to you and your cherished companion.

THE END

ACKNOWLEDGMENTS

Yvonne, Stephanie, Amy, Brittany, Sandy, Jenna, Rose Ann, Meredith, Karen, Jennifer and Jason, Phung and Chi, Kellie, Laura thank you for your friendship, support, and love. Your presence in our lives means more than words can express. We will always be grateful to Instagram for bringing us together.

Molly Martin thank you for telling me to get the book "SIGNS: The Secret Language of the Universe" by Laura Lynne Jackson and for checking in on me consistently every few days to make sure I was okay. Through this book, we've discovered a language that connects us with Kingston and for that we will be forever grateful.

My friends and cheerleaders, Audrey Wu, Jennifer Gudeman, Greg Divis, CG Hintmann, Elise Lapke, Melissa Falcone, Jamie Jansson, Scott Goedeke, Michelle Sondker, Debbie Lanemann for always believing in me and my career even when I didn't have it for myself.

Dr. Steven Glaser, Lexi, Mackenzie, and everyone at Creve Coeur Animal Hospital thank you. Your exceptional care for our kids has been a cornerstone of our lives. Your compassion, from managing routine check-ups to addressing emergencies, has been invaluable. Your care and time in explaining treatments, bloodwork and medications have not only kept our pets healthy but also reassured us as a family.

"University of Illinois entire team, and especially Ashley Vahling, who went above and beyond in their care for our Edmond and in how they loved on us. Truly, sincerely, thank you."

ABOUT THE AUTHOR

Erika Sinner is a CEO, a compassionate advocate, and the guiding force behind Directorie™, a company dedicated to propelling life science organizations forward in bringing vital products to market. With a career spanning nearly two decades, Erika's innovative spirit has fostered successful teams and elevated brands within the pharmaceutical industry.

Erika's unwavering commitment to reimagining possibilities extends far beyond the boardroom; she's a woman of action, unafraid to confront societal gaps head-on. Her determination to foster empathetic solutions shines in both her professional and personal life. Erika stands not only as an exceptional CEO but also a devoted wife, a passionate supporter of animals, and leading organizations with compassion.

Fueled by her experience in grief, Erika recognized an unaddressed dimension of pet loss, prompting her to shine a light on this often-overlooked facet of the human experience. Through her compelling storytelling, she empowers us to create a world that better supports one another in times of sorrow. Erika's vision includes advocating for the inclusion of pet bereavement leave in organizational policies, sparking a wave of empathy-driven change and leadership.

Erika's remarkable capacity to effortlessly blend approachable friendless with strong support has left an enduring impact on those fortunate enough to cross her path. Her courage in openly sharing her personal journey of loss and vulnerability serves as a guiding light of hope for individuals navigating their own challenges. This book, a reflection of Erika's spirit, will resonate with your heart and guide you toward meaningful action in the face of adversity. Erika is not merely an author; she's a catalyst for healing and transformation.